THE AVRO
Vulcan
A HISTORY

THE AVRO
Vulcan
A HISTORY

PETER G. DANCEY

TEMPUS

First published 2007

Tempus Publishing Limited
The Mill, Brimscombe Port,
Stroud, Gloucestershire, GL5 2QG
www.tempus-publishing.com

British Library Cataloguing in Publication Data.
A catalogue record for this book is available from the British Library.

ISBN 978 07524 4089 7

Typesetting and origination by Tempus Publishing Limited.
Printed in Great Britain.

Contents

Acknowledgements

The photographs used in this work have been collected over more than a decade since I began aviation writing in 1995; unfortunately there are some whose origins are unclear. A number are from the now defunct Part Works; all others are detailed except where they originate from my personal archives. Should any material be inadvertently unaccredited, reproduced without permission, or copyright infringed, I offer my unreserved apologies.

To all contributors I express my gratitude, in particular those I have been unable to contact. To anyone I have forgotten, I offer my unreserved apologies.

Peter G. Dancey
January 2007

Introduction

The Vickers Valiant 'V' class bombers formed Britain's first post-Second World War nuclear deterrent force under the control of Bomber Command. The prototype serial WB210 flew on 18 May 1951 and the first squadron of Valiant B.1s was formed in January 1955. Armed with conventional bombs, the type saw operational service during the Suez Crisis in 1956 and was also used in Britain's first atomic and thermo-nuclear bomb tests in 1956–57. Total Valiant production amounted to 104 aircraft.

The second of the RAF's trio of V-bombers, with its (at the time) unconventional delta-wing configuration, was the Avro Vulcan, and the third was the Handley Page Victor, with its equally unconventional but still highly effective crescent wing.

The prototype Avro 698 Vulcan serial VX770 first flew on 30 August 1952, and the type became operational less than five years later with No.83 Squadron at RAF Waddington, Lincolnshire. The first of the twenty-five Vulcan B.1s to enter production, serial XA889, flew in February 1955, twelve months ahead of the Handley Page Victors. A total of 136 Avro Vulcans were built, including two prototypes.

By 1956 Avro had produced many design changes, which resulted in B.1 production being halted, and its eventual replacement by the B.2 version. The changes included new electronic countermeasure equipment (ECM) and tail radar, new electrical power plant elevons (replacing the separate elevator and ailerons), and the new larger Phase 2C wing and uprated Olympus 200 series engines. There was an additional 25–30 per cent increase in range and a significant gain in operational altitude (the prototype B.2 reached 61,500ft in March 1959). After extensive development, the first B.2 entered RAF service in 1960 and the twenty-nine existing B.1s were partially modified to B.2 standard between 1960 and 1963, and then re-designated as B.1As.

The intended role of the V-bomber, and in particular the Avro Vulcan, was to implement Britain's nuclear deterrent, a role it performed well despite the Government's ever-changing nuclear weapon policy. The original device was the 10,000lb free-fall Blue Danube, but with the introduction of ever more sophisticated Soviet surface-to-air missiles this early model quickly became outdated; both the Blue Streak ballistic missile and the Blue Steel stand-off missile came to be seen as the Vulcan's main armament. The Avro Co. were made prime contractors for Blue Steel, and trials were carried out culminating in successful firings from a B.1 in 1959. The missiles were first carried operationally by modified B.2s in 1963, with new bomb doors and a modified bomb-bay; these airframes were then re-designated as B.2A. Subsequently, an improved version Blue Steel Mk.2 was cancelled in 1959 along with the Blue Streak project in 1960. The replacement was to be the American Skybolt missile, for which all future B.2s were modified with a strengthened wing structure, under-wing hard-points and Olympus 301 engines. In 1962 the Americans cancelled Skybolt in favour of the submarine-borne Polaris missiles as the two countries' primary nuclear deterrent. This decision signalled the end for the British V-bomber airborne nuclear deterrent.

Nevertheless, as Polaris was not due to enter service until the late 1960s it was decided that the RAF should still maintain the deterrent using their recently acquired Mk.1 Blue Steel and the new low-level British-developed H-bomb. The advent of further Soviet SAM development negated the Vulcan's high-level flight advantage and the bomber was forced into a new low-level role for which it was never designed but handled with aplomb.

The re-roled bombers also received a new livery in 1964, changing from the anti-flash all-white to a grey-green camouflage on the upper surfaces. By 1966 the Vulcans had been fitted with a terrain-following radar (TFR) which assisted high-speed, low-level (below 1,000ft) sorties to targets underneath enemy radar surveillance. By the time Polaris entered service in 1969, low-level operations had proved so successful that it was decided to keep sixty Vulcans operational, the airplane reverting to a free-fall bombing role. In fact, it continued in service until the multi-role Panavia Tornado GR.1 replaced it in 1982. Over the next few years, Vulcans took on various tasks. They were used by No.27 Squadron when they reverted to high-level strategic and maritime reconnaissance missions and at this stage the aircraft was re-designated as B.2 (MRR). During its career as a B.1 aircraft, serial XA903 was used to carry out Aerospatiale/BAC Concorde SST and Panavia Tornado RB.199 engine trials, while it was also one of the aircraft based in Cyprus on standby during the Turkish/Greek Cypriot troubles. In 1979 the aircraft were painted all over in matt camouflage to reduce their vulnerability to fighter attack at low level.

After twenty-seven years of service, the twilight of its career saw the Vulcan called on to go to war in the South Atlantic during the Falklands conflict. Of those airplanes available, only five were fitted with the Skybolt-strengthened hard-points, which were essential to allow fitment of the latest ECM radar jammer. Various parts and modifications were embedded in record time to permit the first of the Black Buck missions to be flown on 30 April 1982. The missions were flown from Ascension Island, 4,000 miles from the Falklands, and so involved complex in-flight refuelling procedures using eleven H.P. Victor tankers. The first mission achieved a direct hit on Port Stanley's runway, and although it remained operational for Argentine forces the psychological damage inflicted was of great importance. The sixteen-hour flight served as a warning to Argentina that it, too, was vulnerable to attack by British bombers. Black Bucks One, Two and Three carried twenty-one 1,000lb free-fall bombs, whereas Four, Five and Six used American-supplied, wing-mounted Shrike anti-radar missiles. The final Black Buck mission (Seven) carried a mixture of conventional and anti-personnel bombs.

After the Falklands War two more Vulcan squadrons were disbanded, leaving only No.50 Squadron, from where six Vulcans were converted to tankers and re-designated B.2(K) as an interim measure until the new BAC VC.10Ks arrived in 1984. The last Vulcan 'scramble' took place on 14 March 1984, with No.50 Squadron disbanding on the 31st of that month. Vulcans XL426 and XH558 were kept in airworthy condition by the RAF for display purposes with the latter airplane continuing for a number of years, until it arrived at its final resting place at Bruntingthorpe Aerodrome, Leicestershire, just after 1.30 p.m. on Tuesday 23 March 1993, guided in by a 'period' follow-me Standard Vanguard pick-up truck. Following the shut-down of its engines for the last time as an RAF aircraft, a brief hand-over ceremony took place in front of the control tower and the airplane Servicing Form 700 was presented to its new owner, David Walton.

Earlier in the day, just after 10.10 a.m. at RAF Waddington, Lincolnshire, XH558 had started its engines and moved out from near the control tower to taxi towards the end of runway 21 and prepare for take-off. Following the customary engine run-ups prior to take-off, it was soon rolling down the runway for the last time at Waddington, its nose pointing high as it climbed out in the manner characteristic of Vulcan bombers.

On levelling out after becoming airborne, XH558 opened its bomb-bay to show the doors adorned with 'FAREWELL' in a heartfelt message to its enthusiastic fans below. Piloted by Squadron Leader Paul Millikin, XH558 appeared over the twin-towers of Lincoln Cathedral to bid a final farewell to the historic city at approximately 12.30 p.m., and within minutes flew across Waddington again for the last time, before heading off to Bruntingthorpe where the reception committee included a dual-seat Supermarine Spitfire Tr.9 serial ML407 from Duxford, and two former BAe (English Electric) Lightning F.6s, serials XR728 and XS904 (both the property of the Lightning Preservation Group), that had already taken up residency at the airfield on the type's retirement.

A former Vulcan Display Flight pilot, Squadron Leader Millikin flew slowly over Bruntingthorpe for a final check on the runway, before landing the aircraft, streaming its massive brake parachute, and coming to rest in full view of a large crowd in front of the control tower, finally shutting down its four Olympus engines.

It is now more than ten years since that momentous day, and in spite of the hopes and aspirations of its current owners, British Aviation Heritage, Vulcan B.2 XH558 with civil registration G-VLCN has not flown since. Short on airframe hours and requiring a major overhaul costing several million pounds, it is highly unlikely that it ever will. Subsequently, the Vulcan Operating Co., working in conjunction with Marshall Aerospace, was optimistic that XH558 would take to the air again, with a first flight planned for 2006.

Avro Vulcan B.2, serial XL426 (G-VJET), owned by the Vulcan Restoration Trust at Southend, finds itself in a similar situation. XL426 is one of the initial batch of twenty-four B.2s ordered on 25 February 1956; it entered RAF service on 7 September 1962 with No.83 Squadron, then served successively with Nos 27, 50 and 617 Squadrons plus 230 OCU. The airplane had a fairly uneventful service career, being generally reliable and dependable throughout.

CAA requirements for both XH558 and XL426 call for a major contractor with type experience to take charge of the airframes before they can be issued with a Certificate of Airworthiness. Upon certification they can take to the air again. In a last desperate endeavour to save XL426 and achieve certification, the Vulcan Memorial Flight Supporters' Club was formed in March 1990. Towards the end of 1990, BAF Engineering Ltd at Southend Airport, Essex, carried out a survey of the airplane and, considering the amount of time it had spent in the open, found it to be in very good condition. All four engines were run up at low power for fifteen minutes and all systems functioned satisfactorily. BAF's conclusion was that, 'given adequate time and funds, the aircraft is a viable proposition'. Nevertheless, it is now accepted by all concerned that it is unlikely XL426 will ever fly again…

Opposite: The Avro Type 698, serial VX770, prototype long-range delta-winged strategic bomber made its maiden flight at Avro's Woodford Aerodrome on 30 August 1952 in its distinctive all-white colour scheme, national markings, and with its 'Avro' badge proudly displayed high on the tail fin. (Mike Hooks)

Famous Vulcans

VX770   prototype, delivered August 1952
VX777   second prototype, completed September 1953, later converted to prototype B.2
XA889   first production B.1, delivered 4 February 1955
XA894   engine test-bed for Olympus 320 as part of the E.E./BAC TSR 2 programme
XA896   engine test-bed for Bristol Siddeley BS 100 as part of the Hawker P.1124 programme
XA900   last B.1 variant, scrapped 1986
XA903   test-bed for Concorde SST and Panavia Tornado engines. Initial Blue Steel trials
           aircraft
XH533   first production B.2, first flight 19 August 1958
XH558   last Vulcan in RAF service, sold to private owner March 1993
XL320   flew the 500,000th accumulated Vulcan flying hours on 18 December 1981
XL321   most individual Vulcan aircraft flying hours, 6,952 hours
XM607   flew 'Black Buck One', attack on Port Stanley, Falklands Airfield on 30 April/1 May
           1982, plus two other Black Buck missions
XM657   last production B.2

Serial VX770 was flown to Farnborough two days after its first flight by Avro's chief test pilot 'Roly' Falk for the prototype nuclear bomber's first public display. (Mike Hooks)

The 'perfect delta' was powered by four Rolls-Royce Avon engines for its maiden flight, but was later fitted with Armstrong Siddeley Sapphires 6s before test model R-R Conway Mk.5s were fitted at the Rolls-Royce airfield at Hucknall, Nottinghamshire. R-R Conway tests were flown during the summer of 1958. Unfortunately, VX770 disintegrated in the air during a high-speed flypast at RAF Syerston during Battle of Britain Day on 20 September that year. (Mike Hooks)

The second Type 698, serial VX777, with Bristol Olympus engines, joined VX770 and the H.P. 80 Victor at Farnborough in 1953. VX770 on the left is seen in company with its stable-mate VX777 on the right. In addition to the H.P. 80, various pieces of ground equipment and motor vehicles of the era can be seen, in particular an RAF 'Queen Mary' to the left of the small Nissan-hut-type building; this special vehicle was used for transporting aircraft fuselages and wings by road. A service refuelling bowser is adjacent to the Victor. (Mike Hooks)

Pictured landing with airbrakes extended at the 1953 Farnborough Air Show, serial VX777, is fitted with the broader-chord wing, adopted to improve aerodynamics, handling and general performance. A twin-rotor Bristol 173 helicopter, forerunner to the Bristol Type 192 Belvedere (the first twin-rotor helicopter to enter service with the RAF), can be seen on the extreme left. (Mike Hooks)

The first completed Vulcan B.1s were delivered to No.230 OCU at RAF Waddington in 1955 and the first squadron, No.83, was equipped there two years later. The squadron's aircraft were delivered in all-white anti-flash finish. This aircraft, in aluminium finish, a 'borrowed' 230 OCU machine, is already undergoing its 'after flight' checks, even though the crew have only just disembarked. No less than four refuelling bowsers are in attendance and the oxygen replenishment trolley is in front of the aircraft. (*Take Off*, Part Works)

Opposite above: Both Vulcan Type 698 prototypes were used extensively for early manufacturers' trials and VX770 early engine development work. Here both airplanes are airborne together and the trailing edge elevator tabs and ailerons of the lead aircraft can just be seen at the top of the picture. (Mike Hooks)

Opposite below: Early production Vulcan B.1 with straight delta wing, serial XA889, in RAF colours with its high-visibility 54in roundel at Avro's test airfield, Woodford, Chester, in September 1955. For ease of servicing the big delta bomber all access hatches opened underneath the airframe. (Mike Hooks)

Early 230 OCU deliveries to Waddington included Vulcan B.1 serials XA902, XA896 and XA895; these 1957 aircraft were finished in a nuclear anti-flash white colour scheme before being loaned to No.83 Squadron for operational use, with no unit markings but the City of Lincoln badge on the tail. Three E.E. Canberra light-bombers can be seen parked opposite. (Mike Hooks)

Opposite: Completed in 1957, Vulcan B.1, serial XA894, was used as the engine test-bed for the Bristol Olympus 22R for the cancelled E.E./BAC/TSR2 programme. Unfortunately, this Vulcan was destroyed at Patchway by a ground fire on 3 December 1962. (Mike Hooks)

Waddington hangars became a hive of activity in September 1957 as early Vulcan B.1 bombers underwent service acceptance checks by RAF engineers before entering front-line squadron service. This was normal procedure as new types were taken on charge. (*Lincolnshire Echo*)

Part of the acceptance checks involved checking the capacious bomb-bay and bomb-release mechanisms. (*Lincolnshire Echo*)

Vulcan Roll Call

Prototypes	Date completed	Squadron/unit	Remarks
VX770 698	Aug. 1952	trials	crashed Syerston structural failure, 20 Sep. 1958
VX777 698	Sep. 1953	trials	converted to prototype Mk.2 – scrapped Jul. 1963

Vulcan B. Mk.1/1A (thirty B.1s were modified to B.1A standard beginning March 1960)

XA889 B.1	Feb. 1955	trials	scrapped in 1971
XA890 B.1	1955	trials	scrapped in 1971
XA891 B.1	1955	trials	crashed near Hull, 24 Jul. 1959
XA892 B.1	1955	trials/inst	scrapped in 1972
XA893 B.1	1956	trials	scrapped in 1962
XA894 B.1	1957	trials	destroyed by ground fire, 3 Dec. 1962
XA895 B.1/A	Aug. 1956	230/trials	sold as scrap, 1 Sep. 1968
XA896 B.1	Mar. 1957	230/83/44/trials	scrapped in 1966
XA897 B.1	Jul. 1956	230/trials	crashed at Heathrow Airport, 1 Oct. 1956
XA898 B.1	Jan. 1957	230/inst	scrapped in 1971
XA899 B.1	Feb. 1957	trials/inst	scrapped in 1973
XA900 B.1	Mar. 1957	230/101/inst	scrapped in 1986
XA901 B.1	Apr. 1957	230/44/83/inst	scrapped in 1972
XA902 B.1	May 1957	230/engine trials	damaged during landing, Feb. 1958, scrapped in 1963
XA903 B.1	May 1957	trials	scrapped in 1980
XA904 B.1/A	Jul. 1957	83/44/inst	crash-landed, March 1961, later scrapped
XA905 B.1/A	Jul. 1957	83/44/230/inst	scrapped in 1974
XA906 B.1/A	Aug. 1957	83/44	sold as scrap, Nov. 1968
XA907 B.1/A	Aug. 1957	83/44	sold as scrap, May 1968

Vulcan B. Mk.1/1A	Date completed	Squadron/unit	Remarks
XA908 B.1	Sep. 1957	83	crashed in Michigan, USA, 24 Oct. 1958
XA909 B.1/A	Oct. 1957	101/50	crashed Anglesey (engine failure) 16 Jul. 1964
XA910 B.1/A	Oct. 1957	101/230/50/44/inst	scrapped
XA911 B.1/A	Dec. 1957	83/230	sold as scrap, Nov. 1968
XA912 B.1/A	Dec. 1957	101	scrapped
XA913 B.1/A	Dec. 1957	101	sold as scrap, May 1968
XH475 B.1/A	Feb. 1958	101/Wad/inst	scrapped in 1969
XH476 B.1/A	Feb. 1958	101/44	sold as scrap, Jan. 1969
XH477 B.1/A	Feb. 1958	83/44/50	crashed in Scotland, 12 Jun. 1963
XH478 B.1/A	Mar. 1958	83/44/trials/inst	scrapped
XH479 B.1/A	Mar. 1958	83/44/inst	scrapped in 1973
XH480 B.1/A	Apr. 1958	83/44	sold as scrap, 1968
XH481 B.1/A	Apr. 1958	101/44/inst	scrapped in 1977
XH482 B.1/A	May. 1958	617/50/101	scrapped in 1968
XH483 B.1/A	May. 1958	617/50/inst	scrapped in 1977
XH497 B.1/A	May. 1958	617/50	scrapped in 1969
XH498 B.1/A	Jun. 1958	617/50/inst	scrapped
XH499 B.1/A	Jul. 1958	617/50/44/trials	scrapped
XH500 B.1/A	Aug. 1958	617/50/inst	scrapped in 1977
XH501 B.1/A	Sep. 1958	617/44/50	sold as scrap, 1968
XH502 B.1/A	Nov. 1958	617/50/inst	scrapped
XH503 B.1/A	Dec. 1958	83/44	sold as scrap, 1968
XH504 B.1/A	Dec. 1958	230/inst	scrapped
XH505 B.1/A	Mar. 1959	230/617/50/inst	scrapped
XH506 B.1/A	Apr. 1959	101/617/50	sold as scrap, 1968
XH532 B.1/A	Mar. 1959	230/101	sold as scrap, 1968

Vulcan B. Mk.2	Date completed	Squadron/unit	Remarks
XH533	Aug. 1958	trials	sold as scrap, 1970
XH534 MRR	Jul. 1959	trials/27	sold as scrap, 1982
XH535	May 1960	trials	crashed near Andover, 11 May 1964
XH536	Jul. 1959	trials/Wad	crashed in Wales (TFR trial) 11 Feb. 1966
XH537 MRR	Aug. 1959	trials/230/27	Abingdon 1983 – front fuselage Bournemouth Museum
XH538	Sep. 1959	trials/230/27/35	sold as scrap, 1981
XH539	Sep. 1959	trials/inst	scrapped
XH554	Oct. 1959	83/230/inst	scrapped

Vulcan B. Mk.2	Date completed	Squadron/unit	Remarks
XH555	Jun. 1961	27/230/trials	scrapped 1971
XH556	Sep. 1961	27/230/inst	scrapped
XH557	May 1960	trials/Cot/Wad/Akr	sold as scrap 1982
XH558 MRR/K2	Jun. 1960	230/27/50	last Vulcan in service, sold in Mar. 1993
XH559	Jul. 1960	230	sold as scrap, Jan. 1982
XH560 MRR/K2	Sep. 1960	230/12/27/50	scrapped
XH561 K2	Oct. 1960	230/Wad/Cot/Akr	scrapped
XH562	Nov. 1960	230/35/50/9/101	scrapped 1984
XH563 MRR	Dec. 1960	83/12/230/27	scrapped
XJ780 MRR	Jan. 1961	83/12/230/27	sold as scrap, 1982
XJ781	Feb. 1961	83/12/230	damaged during landing and SOC May 1973
XJ782 MRR	Feb. 1961	83/12/230/27	scrapped
XJ783	Mar. 1961	83/9/230/35/617	sold as scrap, 1982
XJ784	Mar. 1961	trials/230/9/44/101	sold as scrap, 1982
XJ823 MRR	Apr. 1961	27/35/230/9/27/50	sold Jan. 1983 Solway Aviation Soc. Carlisle
XJ824	May 1961	27/9/230/35/44/101	Imperial War Museum, Duxford – Mar. 1982
XJ825 MRR/K2	Jul. 1961	27/35/230/27/50	scrapped 1992
XL317 Blue Steel	Jul. 1961	trials/617/230	scrapped
XL318 Blue Steel	Aug. 1961	617/230/27	RAF Museum, Hendon, as 8733M in Feb. 1982
XL319 Blue Steel	Oct. 1961	617/230/35/44	sold Jan. 1983
XL320 Blue Steel	Nov. 1961	617/83/27/230	sold as scrap, 1981
XL321 Blue Steel	Jan. 1962	617/27/230/44/35/50	scrapped
XL359 Blue Steel	Jan. 1961	617/27/230/35	sold as scrap, 1982
XL360 Blue Steel	Feb. 1962	617/230/35/101	sold Jan. 1983 Midland Air Museum, Coventry
XL361 Blue Steel	Mar. 1962	617/230/27/35/9	grounded (accident) Goose Bay, Jun. 1982
XL384 Blue Steel	Mar. 1962	230/Sca/Wad/inst	heavy-landing Aug. 1971, SOC May 1985
XL385 Blue Steel	Apr. 1962	9/Sca	involved in ground fire, SOC Apr. 1967
XL386 Blue Steel	May 1962	9/230/44/101/50	scrapped
XL387 Blue steel	May 1982	230/101/50	sold as scrap, 1983
XL388 Blue Steel	Jun. 1962	9/230/617/44	sold as scrap, 1985
XL389 Blue Steel	Jul. 1962	230/617/9/44/101	sold a scrap, 1981
XL390 Blue Steel	Jul. 1962	9/230/617	crashed Glenview, USA (display) 12 Aug. 1978

Vulcan B. Mk.2	Date completed	Squadron/unit	Remarks
XL391 BS/BB	May 1963	trials/9/101/44	sold, Feb. 1983 to a private owner in Blackpool
XL392 Blue Steel	Jul. 1962	83/230/617/35	scrapped
XL425 Blue Steel	Aug. 1962	83/617/27	sold as scrap, 1982
XL426 Blue Steel	Sep. 1962	83/230/617/27/50	sold in Dec. 1986 to the Vulcan Restoration Trust, Southend
XL427 Blue Steel	Sep. 1962	83/617/27/230/9/50/44	scrapped 1986
XL443 Blue Steel	Oct. 1962	83/35	sold as scrap, 1982
XL444 Blue Steel	Oct. 1962	27/230/617/35/9	sold as scrap, 1982
XL445 BS/K2	Nov.1962	27/35/230/44/50	scrapped
XL446	Nov. 1962	27/230/35/617	sold as scrap, 1982
XM569 Blue Steel	Jan. 1963	27/9/50/101/44	sold in Jan. 1983 to the Gloucester Aviation Collection
XM570 Blue Steel	Feb. 1963	27/35/230/617	sold as scrap, 1982
XM571 BS/K2	Feb. 1963	83/27/35/50/617/101	to Gibraltar in May 1984, later scrapped
XM572 Blue Steel	Feb. 1963	83/35/9	sold as scrap, 1982
XM573 Blue Steel	Mar. 1963	83/230/27/44/9	presented to Offut AFB USA, Jun. 1982
XM574 Blue Steel	Jun. 1963	27/230/101/35/617	sold as scrap, 1982
XM575 Blue Steel	May 1963	617/230/101/50/44	sold Jan. 1983 East Midlands Airport Aeropark
XM576 Blue Steel	Jun. 1963	Scampton	crash-landed and struck-off-charge May 1965
XM594 Blue Steel	Jul. 1963	27/101/44	sold Jan. 1983 to the Newark Air Museum
XM595 Blue Steel	Aug. 1963	617/27/35	sold as scrap, 1982
XM596 Fatigue Tests	–	–	scrapped 1972
XM597 BS/BB	Aug. 1963	12/101/44/50/944	Museum of Flight East Fortune – Apr. 1984
XM598 Black Buck	Aug. 1963	12/101/44/50/9	Cosford Aerospace Museum, Jan. 1983
XM599	Sep. 1963	35/101/50/44	sold as scrap, 1982
XM600	Sep. 1963	35/101	crashed near Spilsby (fire) 17 Jan. 1977
XM601	Oct. 1963	9/Coningsby	crashed at Coningsby, 7 Oct. 1964

Veteran Vulcan B.2 BB, serial XM607, completed in December 1963, taking-off from RAF Greenham Common, Berkshire, during its 'at home day' in the late 1960s. At this time the bomber was on the equipment inventory of No.35 Squadron at RAF Cottesmore, Rutland. Now, as veteran of the Falklands 1982 Black Buck missions, it is gate guardian at RAF Waddington, Lincolnshire. (Ron Smith)

Vulcan B. Mk.2	Date completed	Squadron/unit	Remarks
XM602	Nov. 1963	12/9/230/35/101	sold to St Athan Museum Mar. 1983 Avro Woodford
XM603	Nov. 1963	9/50/101/44	sold to BAe Mar.1982 as mock-up for K2
XM604	Nov. 1963	35/Cgy/Cot	crashed at Cottesmore (overshoot), Jan. 1968
XM605	Dec. 1963	9/101/50	presented to Castle AFB, USA, Sep. 1981
XM606	Dec. 1963	12/101/9	presented to Barksdale AFB, USA – Jun. 1982
XM607 Black Buck	Dec. 1963	35/44/9/101	RAF Waddington Gate Guardian, Jan. 1983
XM608	Jan. 1964	Cgy/Cot/Wad	sold as scrap, 1982
XM609	Jan. 1964	12/230/9/44	sold as scrap, 1981
XM610	Feb. 1964	Cgy/Cot/Wad	crashed Wingate (fire) 8 Jan. 1971
XM611	Feb. 1964	9/101	sold as scrap, 1983
XM612	Feb. 1964	9/101/44/trials	Norwich Museum Jan. 1983
XM645	Mar. 1964	230/101/9	crashed in Malta (explosion), Oct. 1975
XM646	Apr. 1964	12/9/101	sold as scrap, 1983
XM647	Apr. 1964	35/9/44/50	scrapped, 1985
XM648	May 1964	9/101/44	sold as scrap, 1982
XM649	May 1964	9/101	sold as scrap, 1982
XM650	May 1964	12/44/50	sold as scrap, 1984
XM651	Jun. 1964	12/101/50	sold as scrap, 1982
XM652	Aug. 1964	9/44/50	scrapped in 1985
XM653	Aug. 1964	9/101/44	sold as scrap, 1981
XM654	Oct. 1964	12/101/50	sold as scrap, 1982
XM655	Nov. 1964	9/101/44/50	sold in Feb. 1984 to a private owner, Wellesbourne Mt.
XM656	Dec. 1964	35/101/9	sold as scrap, 1983
XM657	Jan. 1965	35/101/50/44	last series production aircraft – scrapped

Key

MMR	Maritime Reconnaissance Conversion
BB	Black Buck (Falklands 1982 bombing missions)
BS	Blue Steel – Stand-off bomb
Inst	ground instructional airframe
K.2	air-to-air refuelling conversion
SOC	struck-off-charge
TFR	Terrain Following Radar
Akr	RAF Akrotiri, Cyprus
Cgy	RAF Coningsby, Lincolnshire
Cot	RAF Cottesmore, Rutland
Sca	RAF Scampton, Lincolnshire
Wad	RAF Waddington, Lincolnshire

Vulcan Losses

Airframe	Date	Location	Cause
XA897	1 Oct. 1956	Heathrow	crashed on approach at London HR
VX770	20 Sep. 1958	Syerston	structural failure
XA908	24 Oct. 1958	Michigan, USA	electrical failure
XA891	24 Jul. 1959	near Hull, UK	electrical failure
XA894	3 Dec. 1962	Patchway	ground fire

(XA894 blew up during ground running of the under-fuselage mounted 30,000lb Olympus 320 engine under development for the BAC TSR.2 multi-role aircraft which was subsequently cancelled.)

XH477	12 Dec. 1963	Scotland	not known
XH535	11 May 1964	near Andover, UK	not known
XA909	16 Jul. 1964	Anglesey, North Wales	engine explosion
XM601	7 Oct. 1964	Coningsby, Lincs.	crashed on approach RAF Coningsby
XM576	25 May 1965	RAF Scampton, Lincs.	crash-landed
XH536	11 Feb. 1966	Wales	crashed during TFR trial
XL385	6 Apr. 1967	RAF Scampton, Lincs.	ground fire
XM604	30 Jan. 1968	near RAF Cottesmore	pilot lost control during overshoot
XM610	8 Jan. 1971	Wingate	engine bay fire
XJ781	23 May 1973	Shiraz, Iran	crash-landed
XM645	14 Oct. 1975	Zabbar, Malta	explosion
XM600	17 Jan. 1977	near Spilsby, Lincs.	engine bay fire
XL390	12 Aug. 1978	Glenview, USA	crashed during air display

Serial XA900, completed in March 1957, was the last B.1 variant built and saw service with No.230 OCU and No.101 Squadron along with time as a ground instructional airframe until it was scrapped in 1986. (Mike Hooks)

As the last Vulcan in RAF service until it was sold to private owner David Walton at Bruntingthorpe in March 1993, Vulcan B.2, serial XH558, is seen here in early operational anti-flash white livery. Completed in June 1960, the aircraft served with No.230 OCU, No.27 Squadron, No.50 Squadron, and latterly, until retirement, with the Vulcan Display Flight. (Mike Hooks)

Vulcan B.1, serial XA891, completed in 1955, flew trials until it crashed near Hull on 24 July 1959 after suffering complete electrical failure. (Mike Hooks)

Opposite above: Delivered to No.230 OCU in July 1956, Vulcan B.1, serial XA897, was prepared for a 'flag waving' flight to the Antipodes that year after some trials work, only to crash on its return to London Heathrow Airport on 1 October during an approach in bad weather. (Mike Hooks)

Opposite below: First prototype Vulcan Type 698, serial VX770, shows off its sleek delta profile just seconds before it disintegrated in the air at RAF Syerston Battle of Britain Air Day on 20 September 1958. (Mike Hooks)

Vulcan Survivors

Serial	Variant	Units in allocation order	Location
WZ736	707A	–	Greater Manchester Museum of Science & Industry
WZ744	707C	–	Aerospace Museum, RAF Cosford, Shropshire
XH558	B(K).2	230/27/50	British Aviation Heritage, Bruntingthorpe, Leicestershire
XJ823	B.2 MRR	27/35/230/9/27/50	Carlisle Airport, Cumbria
XJ824	B.2 BS	27/9/230/35/44/101	Imperial War Museum, Duxford, Cambridgeshire
XL318	B.2 BS	617/230/27	RAF Museum, Hendon, north London
XL319	B.2 BS	617/230/35/44	North East Aircraft Museum, Northumberland
XL360	B.2 BS	617/230/35/101	Midland Air Museum, Coventry, Warwickshire
XL361	B.2 BS	617/230/27/25/9	Labrador Heritage Society Goose Bay, Canada
XL391	B.2 BS/BB	trials/9/101/44	Blackpool Airport, Lancashire
XL426	B.2 BS	83/230/617/27/50	Vulcan Restoration Trust, Southend Airport, Essex
XM573	B.2 BS	83/230/27/44/9	SAC Museum, Offut AFB, Nebraska, USA
XM575	B.2 BS	617/230/101/50/44	East Midlands Airport, Visitors Centre
XM594	B.2 BS	27/101/44	Newark Air Museum, Winthorpe, Nottinghamshire
XM597	B.2 BS/BB	12/101/44/50/9/44	Museum of Flight, East Fortune, Scotland
XM598	B.2 BB	12/101/44/50/9	RAF Museum Cosford, Shropshire
XM603	B.2 (B(K).2 prototype)	9/50/101/44	Avro Heritage Society, Woodford Manchester

Vulcan B.1 serials XH475, XH478, and XA909 were all early deliveries to No.101 Squadron when it reformed at RAF Finningley in October 1957. Unfortunately XA909 crashed at Anglesey, Wales, on 16 July 1964 due to an engine explosion. XH475 and XH478 were modified to B.1A standard and served with No.101 Squadron, Nos 83 and 44 Squadrons, Waddington-Wing, as an instructional airframe, on trials and as an instructional aircraft, until they were scrapped in 1969. (Mike Hooks)

Vulcan B.2 serial XJ824, completed in May 1961, served with Nos 27 and 9 Squadrons 230 OCU, and Nos 35, 44 and 101 Squadrons until it was presented to the Imperial War Museum, and was hence relocated to Duxford, Cambridgeshire, in March 1982.

Serial	Variant	Units in allocation order	Location
XM605	B.2	9/101/50	Castle Air Museum, Attwater, California, USA
XM606	B.2	12/101/9	8th Air Force Museum, Barksdale, Louisiana, USA
XM607	B.2 BB	35/44/9/101	RAF Waddington, Lincolnshire (8779M)
XM612	B.2 BB	9/101/44/trials	City of Norwich Aviation Museum, Norwich
XM655	B.2	9/101/44/50	John Littler, Wellesbourne Mountford, Warwick

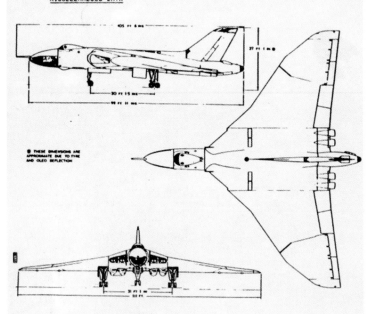

MISCELLANEOUS DATA

ENGINES : 4 off Olympus 20201 turbo-jet 18,000lbs thrust each

WEIGHT : 204,000lbs (91 tons) max. on take-off

SPEED : Max 300kt/0.93 Mach

BOMB LOAD : 21 off 1000lb in standard configuration

FLIGHT DURATION : Approx. 8 hours in standard configuration, no in-flight refuelling

MAXIMUM HEIGHT: Approx.60,000ft

(Vulcan Memorial Supporters' Club booklet)

Cockpit Sections

Serial	Variant	Units in allocation order	Location
XA893	B.1	trials	RAF Museum Cosford, Shropshire
XA903	B.1	trials	Privately owned, Greater London
XH537	B.2 MRR	trials/Con/Wad/Akr	privately owned, Bruntingthorpe, Leicestershire
XH560	B.2 MRR/K.2	230/12/27/50	The Cockpit Collection Rayleigh, Essex
XH563	B.2 MRR	83/12/230/27	Privately owned, Banchory, Scotland
XL388	B.2 BS	9/230/617/44	Blythe Valley Aviation Collection, Suffolk
XL445	B.2 BS/K.2	27/35/23044/50	Blythe Valley Aviation Collection, Suffolk
XM569	B.2 BS	27/9/50/101/44	Jet Age Museum, Staverton, Gloucestershire
XM602	B.2	12/9/230/35/101	Avro Heritage Society, Woodford, Manchester
XM652	B.2	9/44/50	privately owned, Welshpool, Wales

Forty-five Avro Vulcan B.1/B.1As were delivered, followed by eighty-nine re-winged B.2s and B.2As, some with provision to carry the Blue Steel supersonic cruise type air-to-air missile. In 1966 the Vulcan B.2 was re-roled as a low-level penetration-bomber, using a specially developed terrain-following radar Navigational Bombing System (NBS). Navigator/radar crewmen were required to have completed the Bomber Command Bombing School (BCBS) 'Airborne Radar' course at RAF Lindholme, Yorkshire; the unit operated five Handley Page Hastings T.5 aircraft fitted with V-bomber NBS equipment. Early radar training for the V-Force was undertaken by the two Avro Lincoln B.2 squadrons at RAF Hemswell, Nos 83 and 97.

Vulcan B.2 BS/BB, serial XM597, completed in August 1963, touches down its massive air brakes
extended at RAF Greenham Common 'at home day' in the late 1960s. XM597 served variously with
Nos 12, 101, 44, 50 and again with No.44 Squadron until it retired to the Museum of Flight East
Fortune, near Edinburgh, Scotland, in April 1984. (Ron Smith)

Vulcan B.2 BS, serial XL426, following operational service with No.83 Squadron 230 OCU, 617, 27
and 50 Squadrons after a short period as the Vulcan Display Flight display aircraft, was sold in December
1986 to the Vulcan Restoration Society and is now preserved at Southend Airport, Essex. (Ron Smith)

The Vulcan adopted a new role in the twilight of its career, when six B.2s were returned to BAe Woodford in 1982 for conversion to B(K).2 air-to-air refuelling tankers.

Vulcan B(K).2 tanker of No.50 Squadron in 1983 still bears the tail insignia of its previous unit, No.101.

Vulcan B.2, serial XH534, completed in October 1959, served as a trials aircraft and with No.27 Squadron as an MRR variant until its sale as scrap in 1982. At this time No.27 Squadron was using Walt Disney's 'Dumbo' character as the unit badge on the fin.

It was a Vulcan B.2 that, in 1982, made the longest bombing raid in history (since exceeded by USAF Northrop B-2 Spirit stealth bomber operating from Whiteman AFB Missouri) to carry out attacks on the airfield runway at Port Stanley in the Falkland Islands. The aircraft was supported by sixteen H.P. Victor in-flight refuelling tankers operating out of Ascension Island.

Nine Avro Vulcan B.2s were converted and re-roled for operation as long-range strategic maritime reconnaissance aircraft (MRR), and in 1982 six B.2 aircraft were converted to tankers, re-designated B(K).2.

Vulcan B.2s (MRR), which carried a wide range of photographic and electronic sensors, were easily distinguishable from other variants, by the large rectangular RWR antennae enclosure on top of the fin. Vulcan B.2s (MRR) equipped No.27 Squadron at RAF Waddington from November 1973 until March 1982.

Avro Type 707
Research Aircraft

Five Avro Type 707 research aircraft (serials VX784, VX790, WD280, WZ736, WZ744) had been built to test the behaviour of delta wings, particularly at low speeds. The first serial VX784 was completed in August 1949 and, having completed engine trials at Woodford, was dismantled and transported to Boscombe Down, Wiltshire. At Boscombe Down, with the first flight having been carried over from the previous day due to a strong cross-wind, the aircraft, piloted by Flight Lieutenant Eric Esler, took to the air at 7.30 p.m. on 4 September 1949. The flight lasted just twenty minutes. Several more successful flights followed until, tragically, the aircraft crashed on 30 September near Blackbushe, killing Esler.

This tragedy resulted in a temporary halt to the project while the cause of the accident was determined. It was later decided that the delta-wing design had nothing to do with the cause, which was in fact probably pilot error, and so design of the second slow-speed 707 serial VX790 continued, with the addition of an ejection seat for the pilot. VX790, designated 707B, first flew on 6 September 1950 at Woodford piloted by Wing Commander 'Roly' Falk; the successful maiden flight lasted just fifteen minutes. Following many further flights the aircraft proved very successful and thoroughly vindicated Roy Chadwick's delta design. Meanwhile, development of the high-speed aircraft serial WD280, designated 707A, continued. Its first flight was made from Woodford on 14 July 1951 and was the closest Type 707 so far to the final Type 698 design. However, as a result of control problems, the aircraft was fitted with powered flying controls the following year.

It was also decided to build a second 707A serial WZ736, specifically for the Royal Aircraft Establishment at Farnborough. This aircraft was assembled at Bracebridge Heath, near Lincoln, and first flew on 20 February 1953 from RAF Waddington. Rather surprisingly WZ736, on completion, was towed from the Bracebridge works along the main A15 road to Waddington with its airbrakes extended! The road journey, the week before its maiden flight, was made in the depth of winter, with icy roads and snow-covered fields to be negotiated, and on a number of occasions the tiny aircraft and its airfield tow tractor had to pull off the main road to let vehicular traffic pass by.

One further Type 707 aircraft, serial WZ744, a two-seat dual-control variant for crew familiarisation designated the 707C, was built and first flew from Waddington on 1 July the same year.

The 707 programme had generally proved successful, although, as is normal with military research projects, probably more money and effort was expended on the programme than had been originally intended.

First prototype Vulcan VX770, flanked by four Avro 707s, in formation above the English countryside prior to their arrival at the 1952 Farnborough Air Show. (Mike Hooks)

Opposite below: The high-speed Avro 707A, serial WD280, made its maiden flight at Woodford on 14 July 1951 following its attendance at the 1953 Paris Air Show after some general research work with the RAE, including assessment of its handling with powered controls. The plane then left the UK by ship in the spring of 1956 for service with the Australian Aeronautical Research Council at Fishermans Bend, Melbourne. Here it was employed until 1961, on low-speed handling and approach and landing tests. (Mike Hooks)

Having flown for the first time on 3 September 1953, the second Vulcan prototype, serial VX777, leads the VX770, flanked by four Avro 707s serials, WZ736, VX390, WZ744 and WD280, over the 1953 Farnborough Air Show just a few days later.

The first British delta aircraft, Avro 707A, serial VX784, is shown on static display at the 1949 Farnborough Air Show. The aircraft was fitted with a Gloster Meteor jet-fighter cockpit canopy and nose-wheel to hasten its manufacture; it was also used to study delta-wing handling characteristics. (Mike Hooks)

Avro 707A, serial WZ736, with extended vertical tail fairing was designed specifically for use by the RAE at Farnborough. Serialled 7868M, this aircraft is displayed at the Manchester Museum of Science and Industry in the north of England. (*Lincolnshire Echo*)

WZ736 caused much consternation as it held up the traffic on the main A15 truck road in Lincolnshire while being transferred from Bracebridge Heath to Waddington for its first flight in February 1953. (*Lincolnshire Echo*)

The Avro 707C, serial WZ744, was designed as a two-seat trainer. But the cockpit was extremely cramped and the side portholes afforded very little visibility; as a result the aircraft spent most of its life on powered control development work.

Facts, Figures and Technical Details

Total build

Prototypes:	2
Vulcan B.1;	45
Vulcan B.2:	89
Total production:	136

Variants

Type 698:	prototypes
B.1:	series production aircraft powered mainly by Olympus 104 engines
B.1A:	conversion from B1 after fitting ECM equipment in redesigned rear fuselage
B.2:	series production aircraft – redesigned wing of increased area and Olympus 201 or 301 engines
B.2A:	with new bomb doors and modified bomb-bay
B.2 BS:	B.2 airframe modified to carry Blue Steel 100A
B.2 (MRR):	strategic maritime radar reconnaissance conversion
B.2 BB:	B.2 airframe modified for Falklands Black Buck missions
B(K).2:	air-to-air refuelling tanker conversion

Specification: B1

Crew:	5
Length:	29.6m (97ft)
Span:	30.2m (99ft)
Height:	8.1m (26.5ft)
Wing area:	3,400sq. ft approximately
Powerplant:	4 x R-R Olympus 104 (13,400lb thrust) engines

Specification: B2

Crew:	5
Length:	30.5m (100ft) (excluding air-to-air refuelling probe)
Span:	33.8m (111ft)
Height:	8.3m (27ft)
Wing area:	3,964sq. ft
Powerplant:	4 x R-R Olympus 201 or 301 (20,000lb thrust) engines
Maximum speed:	645mph
Operating ceiling:	56,000ft
Typical ranges:	
	3,450 miles (low level without refuelling)
	4,600 miles (medium/high level without AAR)
	8,000 miles (high-low-high with air-to-air refuelling
	– Black Buck missions)
Weight:	100,000lb approximately, empty
Maximum take-off weight:	204,000lb
Stores:	21 x 1,000lb bombs carried internally
Nuclear weapons:	10,000lb free-fall Blue Danube
Missiles:	Blue Streak ballistic missile; Blue Steel stand-off missile; up to 4 x Shrike anti-radar (Black Buck)

Airframe limitations (B2)

Maximum Airframe height:	unrestricted
Maximum operational ceiling:	56,000ft (limited only by oxygen/pressurisation equipment)
Maximum speed:	(above 15,000ft) 330 knots or Mach 0.93 (indicated)
Maximum crosswind limit:	(take-off/landing) 20 knots
Maximum 'G' limit:	
	up to 160,000lb all-up-weight – 2.0 (below Mach 0.89)
	160 to 190,000lb – 1.8 (below Mach 0.89)
	more than 190,000lb – 1.5
Maximum take-off weight:	204,000lb
Maximum normal landing weight:	140,000lb

Normal operating speeds (examples)

Take-off (rotate speed):	up to 150,000lb all-up-weight – 130 knots
170,000lb:	143 knots
190,000lb:	153 knots
204,000lb:	162 knots

Detail around the canopy area of the nose of XM607 features the low-visibility European theatre camouflage and roundel and red cross 'first aid' marking near the appropriate panel. (Modelaid AF1)

This underside view of Vulcan B.2 BS, serial XL426, of No.50 Squadron in 1984 shows the camouflage detail of the underside and also reveals the two small 'day-glo' patches on the trailing edge of the wing which were used to assist aerial refuelling manoeuvres. (Modelaid AF1)

Despite the early loss of serial VX784, the one-third-scale deltas did prove the wing design worked and could support the big bomber. Without them, the Type 698 and ultimately the Avro Vulcan might have proved an unacceptable risk.

It is of interest that all modern multi-role combat types planned to enter service in 2012, including the Saab Gripen, Dassault Rafale, Eurofighter Typhoon, Boeing Raptor and Lockheed Martin F.35 Joint Strike Fighter, feature the delta wing principle. The three former designs also include forward canards for greater stability.

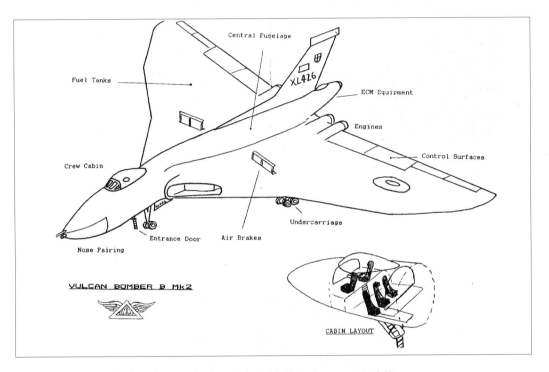

Vulcan Bomber B Mk.2 line drawing. (Vulcan Memorial Flight Supporters' Club)
A History & Guide to Vulcan XL426 'G-VJET. (VMFSC)

Approach speed

Below 120,000lb all-up-weight:	135 knots
150,000lb:	149 knots
180,000lb:	166 knots
204,000lb:	176 knots

Land speed (threshold)

Below 120,000lb all-up-weight:	125 knots
150,000lb:	135 knots
180,000lb:	151 knots
204,000lb:	161 knots

VULCAN'S STRUCTURE AND SYSTEMS

Nose fairing

The fairing houses the Navigational Bombing System (NBS/H2S Mk.9) radar scanner. The upper half is of orthodox metal construction and the lower half is made of a composite material which is transparent to radar signals.

Crew cabin/compartment

The cabin is of circular cross-section with a canopy over the cockpit area, with the Air Bombers blister and entrance door in the underside ahead of the nose-wheel. The crew compartment accommodates a crew of five – two pilots are seated side-by-side at the front of the compartment and three rear crew members (navigator plotter, navigator radar operator and air electronics officer) in the rear of the compartment at a lower level facing rearwards.

The crew compartment was designed in such a way that the pilots sat on Martin-Baker Mk.3 ejection seats under a large metal canopy with portholes either side. In an emergency, the system was designed so that the canopy jettisoned first before the firing of the ejection seats.

For the rear crew, however, the situation was not so good. Should it be necessary to abandon the aircraft then it was up to the three crew members to parachute to safety, after first having extricated themselves from the airplane through the entrance door.

Entrance door

This is situated in the lower fuselage beneath the rear crew compartment. The door opens outwards and entry is by a folding ladder fixed to the door. Operation is by manual and pneumatic means, the latter being used to open the door in flight against the air flow to allow crew emergency exit, the door acting as a windbreak.

Central fuselage

The section is integral with the wing and houses four engines and the bomb-bay. Two ribs form the sidewalls of the bomb-bay, separating it from the engine bays and extend forward to enclose a box structure housing two large fuel tanks. The outer skin covering is of aluminium alloy. Between this structure and the crew cabin is the nose-wheel bay which also houses various radio and radar equipment boxes and two more fuel tanks. To the rear is the tail section which contains the tail radar scanner and electronic counter-measures (ECM) equipment.

Control surfaces

These consist of four elevons (combined ailerons/elevators), each independently operated by its own electro-hydraulic power unit. Two more units power the rudder. Electrically operated rotating slat type air brakes are mounted above and below the engine air intakes on each side of the aircraft.

Flying controls

These consist of pistol grip control handles (similar to a fighter aircraft) and conventional floor rudder pedals for each pilot position. Although the flying controls are powered, artificial feel is provided to give a stick force against movement from the trimmed position.

The aircraft is flown by conventional powered flying controls from either pilot position. Powered flying controls (PFCUs) basically use hydraulic power.

Longitudinal and lateral control is achieved by eight elevons hinged into the wing trailing edge, four on each side. Each elevon is powered by a single PFCU. In the event of PFCU failure, it is arranged in such a way that only one elevon is affected.

The rudder is controlled by two PFCUs – one normal and one back-up.

The electrically operated slab-type airbrakes have three extended positions 35, 55 or 80 degrees. A brake parachute in the tail-cone provides additional braking during the landing run in conjunction with the large tail brake parachute. Streamed at around 135 knots, it was jettisoned when the aircraft slowed to around 50–60 knots.

Undercarriage

This consists of two main-wheel units fitted with a four-wheeled, eight-tyre bogie and a steerable nose-wheel unit fitted with twin wheels. All three units are fully retractable and lie within the normal contours of the aircraft. Wheel brakes are operated by the electrically controlled hydraulic system with a reserve pressure supply provided from two accumulators. Additional braking is made available on landing by deployment of the braking parachute housed in the lower tail section.

Engines/oil

The aircraft is powered by four Olympus 200 Series or 300 Series engines mounted in pairs, inside the main plane section, two either side. Each engine has its own starter motor with air supplied from either a ground starter unit or from a rapid starting system. Access for installation and maintenance is by under-wing hatches thereby maintaining a smooth upper-wing surface and eliminating the requirement for crane lifting equipment. Each engine has its own integral oil system.

The total amount of oil per engine (in the tank and engine) is about 6.5 gallons. An airborne auxiliary power plant (AAPP) provides 200V AC electrical supply in the case of an emergency.

Fuel system

Fuel, normally Avtur or Avtag, is carried in fourteen pressurised tanks – five in each wing and four in the fuselage, with the option of an additional two tanks carried in the bomb-bay. The five bag-type wing tanks are housed within magnesium alloy compartments. The tanks are divided into four groups with each group feeding its own engine. However, a cross-feed system allows the various groups to be inter-connected if required. Each tank is equipped with electric fuel pumps, fuel gauges, maximum-level cut-off switches and refuelling valves. Transfer pumps are also fitted to enable fuel to be moved between tanks to balance the airplane if required. For certain operational roles, additional tanks can be fitted in the bomb-bay. The maximum fuel capacity of the Vulcan (in standard configuration) is 9,260 gallons or approximately 74,080lb depending on the fuel specific gravity – normal S.G. = 0.8. A further 15,900lb could be carried in the bomb-bay tanks.

A nose-mounted air-to-air refuelling probe is connected to the main fuel system. The refuelling rate is approximately 4,000lb/min.

Electrical

Each engine drives one 40kVA alternator which supplies a busbar with 200 volt AC, 3-phase, 400Hz electrical power. From each busbar, a number of transformer rectifier units (TRU) provide the secondary power supplies.

In the event of an AC power supply failure, standby power is supplied by either a ram air turbine (RAT) or the AAPP. Should the main electrical power fail on the aircraft above 40,000ft, the pilot can deploy the RAT, a 17kW air-driven alternator, which drops out of the port underside wing. This will generate sufficient power to maintain vital controls. Below 30,000ft, the pilot can use the AAPP which is a gas turbine engine driving a 40kVA alternator. This is located in the rear of the starboard wheel bay and may be used for ground electrical power should a ground power supply not be available. 28-volt DC power is supplied through two TRUs from four DC busbars. In the event of a single TRU failure, the other supplies all 28-volt services.

Also 112-volt DC power is supplied to the radar from one TRU; a 24-volt battery is connected to a 'vital' busbar at all times.

Hydraulic

The main hydraulic system, containing 12 gallons of hydraulic fluid, provides pressure for raising/lowering the undercarriage, nose-wheel steering, wheel-brakes and opening and closing the bomb-bay doors.

Engine-driven pumps draw fluid from the reservoir and deliver fluid to a main hydraulic gallery at approximately 4,000psi. From the main gallery, fluid is directed at various pressures to the associated systems. A nitrogen system is provided for emergency lowering of the undercarriage.

Pneumatic

Five separate pneumatic systems provide air for various services including engine starting and emergency lowering of the undercarriage.

Electronic counter-measures (ECM)

ECM equipment along with tail radar is contained in the rear fuselage section. The ECM includes large water/glycol-cooled canisters which are part of the 'jamming' systems.

Vulcan NBS/H2S Mk.9 radar

It was on 15 July 1942 that it was decided to incorporate the newly invented 'magnetron' valve in the 'H2S' ('Home Sweet Home', named by Lord Cherwell) navigation equipment already in production. Trials using the lower-powered Klystron valve proved unsatisfactory and it was decided only the magnetron would do. Sadly, the TRE Handley Page Halifax fitted with the first production standard H2S had crashed on 7 June 1942, killing six of Britain's leading experts in this field, and Dr Lovell at the TRE had his work cut out to make up lost ground to permit the flight trials to continue. Trials resumed in mid-July and proved successful, resulting in the development aircraft and three other H2S-equipped Halifaxes being delivered to No.1418 (Gee Development) Flight (that became Bombing Development Unit on 21 July 1942) at Gransden Lodge for service trials, the first two arriving in October 1942. H2S was a development of Gee.

H2S Mk.1 flew its first operational sortie fitted to RAF Pathfinder Short Stirlings and H.P. Halifaxes of Nos 7 and 35 Squadrons during their raid on Hamburg on 28 January 1943. Unfortunately, the equipment did not perform well, with set failures and poor definition predominate problems. 10cm H2S Mk.II followed but still Bomber Command called for a clearer picture and Dr Lovell started work on a 3cm (X-band) set. This equipment made its first flight in a Short Stirling on 11 March 1943 with encouraging results, the narrower beam improving definition considerably. In an effort to overcome production problems, 200 commercially built 10cm sets were converted to 3cm standard. But following a number of problems arising during a series of attacks on Berlin being blamed on these H2S sets, it was decided to equip six Avro Lancasters of the Pathfinder Force with experimental TRE-built 3cm H2S and conduct a properly organised trial, with work starting in September 1943. All six aircraft were ready for operations by mid-November and, after a disappointing first sortie when a number of faults developed, the equipment worked well with results far above expectations. H2S Mk.III was now available and a success.

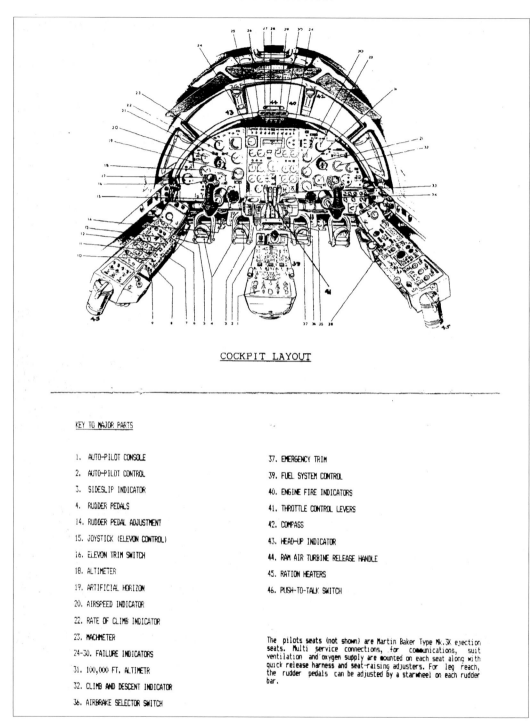

COCKPIT LAYOUT

KEY TO MAJOR PARTS

1. AUTO-PILOT CONSOLE

2. AUTO-PILOT CONTROL

3. SIDESLIP INDICATOR

4. RUDDER PEDALS

14. RUDDER PEDAL ADJUSTMENT

15. JOYSTICK (ELEVON CONTROL)

16. ELEVON TRIM SWITCH

18. ALTIMETER

19. ARTIFICIAL HORIZON

20. AIRSPEED INDICATOR

22. RATE OF CLIMB INDICATOR

23. MACHMETER

24-30. FAILURE INDICATORS

31. 100,000 FT. ALTIMETR

32. CLIMB AND DESCENT INDICATOR

36. AIRBRAKE SELECTOR SWITCH

37. EMERGENCY TRIM

39. FUEL SYSTEM CONTROL

40. ENGINE FIRE INDICATORS

41. THROTTLE CONTROL LEVERS

42. COMPASS

43. HEAD-UP INDICATOR

44. RAM AIR TURBINE RELEASE HANDLE

45. RATION HEATERS

46. PUSH-TO-TALK SWITCH

The pilots seats (not shown) are Martin Baker Type Mk.3K ejection seats. Multi service connections, for communications, suit ventilation and oxygen supply are mounted on each seat along with quick release harness and seat-raising adjusters. For leg reach, the rudder pedals can be adjusted by a starwheel on each rudder bar.

Cockpit layout line drawing. (Vulcan Memorial Flight Supporters' Club)
A History & Guide to Vulcan XL426 'G-VJET. (VMFSC)

Front cockpit and instrument panel.

The pilot's position and controls; considering the size of the aircraft the Vulcan's cockpit is very cramped. Both crew members are Squadron Leader pilots of the Vulcan Display Flight team.

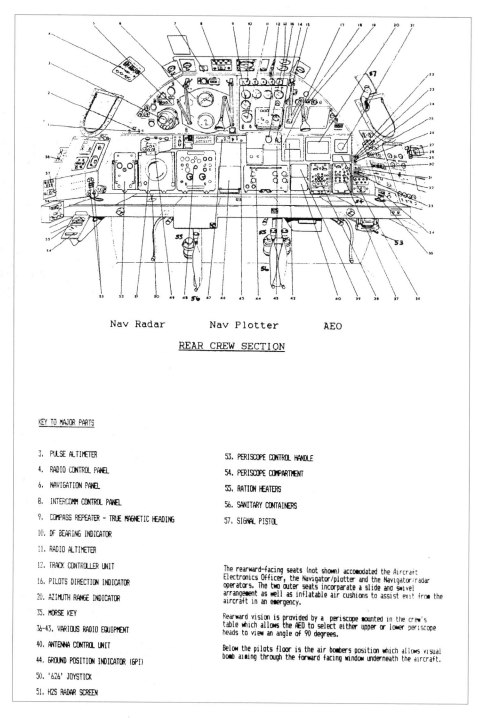

Nav Radar   Nav Plotter   AEO

REAR CREW SECTION

KEY TO MAJOR PARTS

3. PULSE ALTIMETER

4. RADIO CONTROL PANEL

6. NAVIGATION PANEL

8. INTERCOMM CONTROL PANEL

9. COMPASS REPEATER - TRUE MAGNETIC HEADING

10. DF BEARING INDICATOR

11. RADIO ALTIMETER

12. TRACK CONTROLLER UNIT

16. PILOTS DIRECTION INDICATOR

20. AZIMUTH RANGE INDICATOR

35. MORSE KEY

36-43. VARIOUS RADIO EQUIPMENT

40. ANTENNA CONTROL UNIT

44. GROUND POSITION INDICATOR (GPI)

50. '626' JOYSTICK

51. H2S RADAR SCREEN

53. PERISCOPE CONTROL HANDLE

54. PERISCOPE COMPARTMENT

55. RATION HEATERS

56. SANITARY CONTAINERS

57. SIGNAL PISTOL

The rearward-facing seats (not shown) accomodated the Aircraft Electronics Officer, the Navigator/plotter and the Navigator/radar operators. The two outer seats incorporate a slide and swivel arrangement as well as inflatable air cushions to assist exit from the aircraft in an emergency.

Rearward vision is provided by a periscope mounted in the crew's table which allows the AEO to select either upper or lower periscope heads to view an angle of 90 degrees.

Below the pilots floor is the air bombers position which allows visual bomb aiming through the forward facing window underneath the aircraft.

Rear Crew Section line drawing. (Vulcan Memorial Flight Supporters' Club)
A History & Guide to Vulcan XL426 'G-VJET. (VMFSC)

Above: Rear crew comprised the navigator plotter, navigator/radar and air electronics officer. They faced rearward and in an emergency, not having ejection seats, they had to vacate the bomber through the entry hatch. (*Lincolnshire Echo*)

Right: Vulcan B.2, serial XM607, tail fairing detail encapsulates the types ECM suite. (Modelaid AF1)

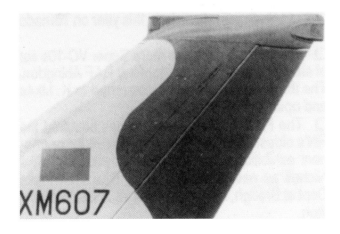

Right: Fin and rudder detail of the same aircraft. (Modelaid AF1)

The TRE now started work on a 1.25cm H2S, the Lion Tamer (later designated H2S Mk.VI), and early in 1944 also started refining H2S Mk.III by fitting an enlarged scanner, the revised equipment known as Whirligig H2S. After several changes of plan it was decided a straightforward development of H2S Mk.III to Mk.IV standard should also go ahead at the same time, and operational trails would be held to ascertain which gave the best results. Comparative trials began in July 1944 and, as experts predicted it was the Mk.IV that worked the best. The Mk.VI was unsatisfactory under operational conditions and the Mk.111F with 6ft scanner was retained for interim use by the Pathfinders, though in practice it remained in general use, after the war.

Post-war, further H2S development centred around the equipment intended for the V-bombers. This used H2S Mk.9 high-definition radar for basic information which was fed, with drift and ground speed inputs from Green Satin Pulse Doppler radar, to the Navigation and Bombing Computer (NBC) Mk.2A.

Avro Vulcan B.Mk 1

The production Vulcan B.Mk 1 introduced a larger area wing, with an extended, slightly drooped leading edge and a slight kink. This reduced transonic buffet. A visual bomb aiming blister was added under the nose.

Avro Vulcan B.Mk 1A

The surviving Vulcan B.Mk 1s were upgraded to B.Mk 1A standard by the addition of ECM in a bulged tailcone. These aircraft entered service in November 1960 and equipped the Waddington wing until 1965.

Avro Vulcan B. Mk 2

The Vulcan B.Mk 2 introduced a new large span wing with a dramatically kinked leading edge, together with uprated Olympus engines and comprehensive ECM equipment for improved performance and penetrability at high level.

Avro Vulcan B.Mk 2BS

Vulcan B.Mk 2s converted to carry the Avro 'Blue Steel' stand-off missile were designated B.Mk 2BS and served with the Scampton wing. When 'Blue Steel' was withdrawn they reverted to standard configuration.

(*Take Off*, Part Works)

Vulcan Variants

Vulcan B. Mk.1

The first production Avro Vulcan B.1 was first flown on 4 February 1955. Beginning with serial XA889, the first production Vulcans were painted silver overall with the bottom section of the large nose radome and the fin top painted black. At first the Vulcan was powered by Olympus Mk.100 engines. But these were later replaced by several other uprated ones; Olympus Mk.101 with 11,000lb thrust, the Mk.102 (12,000lb thrust) and the standard Mk.104 engine rated at 13,400lb thrust.

It is of interest that, despite the horrendous accident at London Heathrow Airport on 1 October 1956, many overseas goodwill and training flights were made by Vulcan B.1 variants, visiting such widely separated places as South America, East Africa, Malaysia, Australia and the United States. Indicative of the bomber's performance are some of the fast times which were recorded on these flights.

In June 1958 a B.1 flew from Ottawa to London, a distance of 5,383km (3,345 miles) in five hours, twenty-one minutes, averaging 1,006km/h (625mph), and in September 1958 another B.1 made the Atlantic crossing from the Labrador coast to the coast of Northern Ireland in three hours at an average speed of 1,043km/h (648mph). In June 1961 another Vulcan B.1 of No.617 Squadron, flown by Squadron Leader M.G. Beavis and his crew, flew non-stop from RAF Scampton, Lincolnshire, to Sydney, Australia, in twenty hours, three minutes, at an average speed of 922km/h (573mph), having been air-refuelled three times by Vickers Valiant tankers operating from Cyprus, Pakistan and Singapore, and in 1962 three Vulcans were simultaneously air-to-air refuelled to Australia in some eighteen hours.

Earlier in April 1959 No.617 Squadron had sent aircraft to the World Congress of Flight at Nellis AFB, Las Vegas, while in October that year three of the unit's aircraft went to New Zealand and after returning via the United States, circumnavigated the world.

Vulcan B. Mk.1A

The increase in engine power created a problem of mild buffeting on the aircraft's wing, giving rise to handling problems. Application of high-g could induce a high-frequency vibration in the outer wings, which in turn would lead to fatigue failure on the wing. Therefore following urgent investigation before the aircraft could enter service, the wing was slightly modified by a reduction of the sweepback from root to semi-span by the introduction of a slight 'kink' in the leading edge. This modification was referred to as the Phase 2 wing. A Vulcan was flown with this modification on 5 October 1955 and found to be satisfactory. Eventually, all the other Mk.1s were modified to this standard.

By April 1957 modified Vulcan B.1s being delivered to the RAF were painted in anti-flash white, with special pale red and blue national markings and serials.

By April 1959 all Avro Vulcans were powered by the Olympus Mk.104 and had an in-flight refuelling probe installed. By this time, forty-five Vulcan B.1s were delivered. During 1961 thirty Mk.1s were fitted with a large ECM installation in a redesigned and greatly enlarged rear fuselage. These modifications resulted in the designation Vulcan B. Mk.1A.

Vulcan B. Mk.2/Mk.2A (BS)

The second prototype, serial VX777, was fitted with a Phase 2C wing whose span grew from 30.2m (99ft) to 33.8m (111ft) and wing area from 3,446sq. ft to 3,965sq. ft in order to provide the same wing loading as the Phase 2 wing at larger weights and a further reduction in thickness/chord ratio. The new wing was necessary due to the more powerful engines, the Olympus Mk.200 that gave 20,000lb thrust. Besides all this, the trailing edge had eight elevons instead of separate ailerons and elevators. Each elevon had an independent power source. The aircraft was fitted with an APU and equipment for the launching of the Blue Steel stand-off bomb or the US Skybolt missile. VX777, the second B.1 prototype, first flew with these modifications on 31 August 1957.

These modifications brought about the new designation Vulcan B. Mk.2/B.2A. This version began to enter service on 1 July 1960 when the first Vulcan B.2, serial XH558, joined No.230 OCU. The first squadron to receive the B.2 was No.83 at RAF Scampton on 23 December 1960 followed by No.27 Squadron and No.617 Squadron in 1961. Eventually, with the introduction of the submarine-launched Polaris missile as the UK's major nuclear deterrent, the Vulcan's role of high-altitude long-range bomber was changed to that of a low-level tactical bomber. It was, therefore, fitted with advanced ECM equipment for better penetration into enemy airspace. Between 1962 and 1964 the Vulcans were re-engined with the 20,000lb thrust Olympus Mk.301 engines.

The switching of the roles and the subsequent modification brought about a slight change in Vulcan designation, that of Vulcan B. Mk.2A. Eighty-nine Vulcans in this mark were produced, the last one being delivered to No.35 Squadron on 14 January 1965. By this time, all Vulcan B. Mk.1s had been withdrawn, although some of them were used in engine installation trials.

Vulcan B.2 (MRR)

During 1973 nine Vulcans were withdrawn from service and converted to the strategic maritime reconnaissance role, giving rise to the B.2 (MRR) variant. Various classified electronic, optical and other sensors, a fin-top RWR, and probably extra fuselage fuel, were installed. The B.2 (MRR) became operational with No.27 Squadron which was reformed on 1 November 1973 at RAF Waddington as a Maritime Radar Reconnaissance (MRR) unit.

Vulcan B.2 BB

When the Vulcan was nearing retirement after thirty years of service with the RAF, to give way to the multi-role Panavia Tornado GR.1, the Falklands conflict broke out in early 1982. The few remaining Vulcans still in front-line service with Nos 44, 50 and 101 Squadrons were required for a long-range attack mission. Ten Vulcans were selected and their air-to-air refuelling equipment was brought to operational standard, having not been used for many years. Eventually only five were on stand-by for possible action associated with the conflict in the South Atlantic. These Vulcans had their light aircraft grey undersides changed to dark sea grey, and their squadron markings removed from their fins. The bombing missions flown from Ascension Island to Port Stanley were code-named 'Black Buck'. In all, seven missions were launched, although two were aborted, between 30 April and 11 June 1982.

Vulcan B(K).2

In order to help the ageing H.P. Victor K.2 tanker fleet support the new Panavia Tornado strike planes and the newly probe-equipped HS Nimrod MR.2s maritime patrol aircraft and Lockheed C-130K Hercules transports, six Vulcans were selected for conversion to in-flight refuelling tankers. A Hose Drum Unit (HDU) was fitted in the former ECM bay at the Vulcan's tail-cone, as well as an extra fuel tank in the bomb-bay. Within fifteen days the Vulcan B(K).2 was cleared by the RAF for operational service. No.50 Squadron operated the Vulcan tankers until it was disbanded at Waddington on 31 March 1984 bringing the end of the Vulcan's front-line service with the RAF, although the Vulcan Display Flight formed in April 1984 from the ex-Vulcan Display Team within No.55 Squadron at Waddington. Flown first was Vulcan B.2 XL426 and then Vulcan B.2 XH558 (re-converted from MRR configuration), seen regularly at air shows throughout the UK until it was disbanded on 21 September 1992 at Waddington.

Avro Vulcan production serial blocks

VX770, VX777	Avro Type 698 prototypes
XA889–XA913	First production Avro Type 698 Vulcan B.1
XH475–XH483	Avro Type 698 Vulcan B.1
XH497–XH506	Avro Type 698 Vulcan B.1
XH532	Avro Type 698 Vulcan B.1

Thirty Vulcan B.1 airframes were converted to Vulcan B.1A standard, including serials: XH500 in 1959; XA895, XA904-5, XA912, XH477, XH481, XH505-7 in 1960; XA907, XA913, XH479, XH483, XH501, XH504 in 1961; XA906, XA909-11, XH475-6, XH478, XH480, XH482, XH497-9, XH502, XH532 in 1967; and XH503 in 1963.

Avro Type 698 Vulcan B.2 serials

XH533–XH539	B.2:	XH534 and XH537 converted to MRR
XH554–XH563	B.2:	XH558, XH560 and XH563 converted to MRR: XH558, 560 and 561 to B(K).2
XJ780–XJ784	B.2:	XJ780 converted to MRR
XJ823–XJ825	B.2:	XJ823 and XJ825 converted to MRR: XJ825 converted to B(K).2
XL317–XL321	B.2:	Blue Steel
XL359–XL361	B.2:	Blue Steel
XL384–XL392	B.2:	Blue Steel; XL391 Black Buck (1982)
XL425–XL427	B.2:	Blue Steel
XL443–XL446	B.2:	XL443, XL444 and XL445 Blue Steel: XL445 converted to B(K).2
XM569–XM576	B.2:	Blue Steel; XM571 also converted to B(K).2
XM594–XM612	B.2:	Blue Steel; XM596 Fatigue Tests; XM597, 598, 607 and 612 Black Buck (1982)
XM645–XM657	B.2:	

Summary of front-line operational service

Vulcan B.1/B.1A served with the following units:
No.83 Squadron at Waddington from July 1957 to August 1960
No.101 Squadron at Finningley and Waddington from January 1958 to January 1968
No.617 Squadron at Scampton from May 1958 to July 1961
No.44 Squadron at Waddington from August 1960 to November 1967
No.50 Squadron at Waddington from August 1961 to November 1966

Vulcan B.2 served with the following units:
No.83 Squadron at Scampton from December 1960 to August 1969
No.27 Squadron at Scampton from April 1961 to March 1972
No.617 Squadron at Scampton from September 1961 to December 1981
No.9 Squadron at Coningsby, Cottesmore, Akrotiri and Waddington from April 1962 to April 1982
No.12 Squadron at Coningsby and Cottesmore from July 1962 to December 1967
No.50 Squadron at Waddington from December 1965 to March 1982
No.44 Squadron at Waddington from November 1967 to December 1982
No.101 Squadron at Waddington from January 1968 to August 1982
No.35 Squadron at Coningsby, Cottesmore, Akrotiri, and Scampton from January 1973 to February 1983
No.27 Squadron at Waddington from November 1973 to March 1982 (MRR variants)
No.50 Squadron at Waddington from March 1982 to March 1984 (B(K).2 variants)

Above: The capacious Vulcan bomb-bay carried up to twenty-one conventional 'iron' bombs alongside its nuclear capacity. One early Avro proposal involved the loading of twenty-four 540lb bombs on tandem pylons under the aircrafts wings. (*Lincolnshire Echo*)

Right: For the Falklands Black Buck One raid on 1 May 1982, Vulcan B.2, serial XM607, was loaded with twenty-one 1,000lb HE 'iron' bombs.

1

Operational Requirements and Specifications

In 1947, with memories of the Second World War still fresh, the Chiefs of Staff declared their belief that the possession of 'weapons of mass destruction' would be the most effective deterrent to war itself. In addition to the possession of a nuclear bomb that would ensure Britain maintained its place at the world's top table, a new and effective delivery system would be needed to replace the Avro Lincoln, essentially a refined and up-engined derivative of the wartime Avro Lancaster. At the time no one knew the importance of this decision and when the Iron Curtain was lowered by the Soviets just a few years later it would play an essential part in maintaining the status quo in the prolonged game of 'cat-and-mouse' that was the Cold War.

At the height of the Cold War, the massive white-painted delta and crescent-winged shaped bombers would thunder off airfields in East Anglia and Lincolnshire or from dispersed sites around the English countryside to reinforce the message to the USSR that nuclear retaliation would be assured and swift if needed.

With the nation exhausted by war the economy seriously weakened, plagued by power cuts and with wartime food rationing still in existence, and with the main priority being the provision of housing and the social welfare of the nation, the British Government nevertheless embarked on a massive leap into the world of nuclear physics and aerodynamics. The prospect of developing a nuclear weapon and new airborne delivery system would have been daunting enough but in order to ensure success no less than four new jet bombers were flown in a very short space of time, of which three achieved quantity production: the Valiant (Vickers), Vulcan (Avro), and Victor (Handley Page).

The 'weapon' had demonstrated its awesome power in August 1945, and on a bleak winter's afternoon on 8 January 1947, six members of the new post-war Labour Government's GEN163 committee met at No.10 Downing Street to reach a momentous decision: Britain would build her own atomic bomb (A-bomb).

Meanwhile, having realised that the piston-engined Avro Lincoln was only slightly better than the wartime Avro Lancaster it was still in the process of replacing, RAF chiefs were already formulating their own plans for a new delivery system for its 'very special' bomb. Bomber Command planners were already looking beyond the gun turrets and the rumble of four Rolls-Royce Merlin or Griffon piston-engines, towards a high-speed, high-altitude, unarmed jet-propelled aircraft, relying on altitude and self-protection electronics to keep itself out of harm's way, to replace the Lincoln.

No sooner had the Second World War ended than it was decided that Britain should build its own A-bomb, and that new jet bomber aircraft would be needed to carry the weapon. (*Take Off*, Part Works)

A 'very special' bomb

By 1945, new bomber needs had crystallised into two Air Staff Requirements (ASR). Operational Requirement OR.229 covered a medium-range aircraft weighing up to 100,000lb, and a more ambitious OR.230 stipulated a limit of 200,000lb for a longer-range airplane. After some revision – not least to take into account Britain's plans for acquisition of the atomic bomb – OR.229 referred to carriage of a single 10,000lb 'special bomb' to a target of 1,730 miles distant, or a still-air range of 3,860 miles. OR.230 looked for 5,000 miles at 575mph with the same load, or a conventional bomb-load of 30,000lb over shorter distances. Both aircraft were to have a crew of five and no defensive armament.

At this time there was little information as to how big Britain's A-bomb would be, so the specification indicated a casing of 24ft 2in long and 5ft in diameter, with its centre-of-gravity 6ft 8in from the nose. It is of interest that, although the devastating power of the 'special weapon' was well known, the requirements included a stipulation that the resultant 'carrier' should be capable of large-scale production in the event of war.

Discussion of the two ORs in committee on 17 December 1946 reached the inevitable conclusion: OR.229 was just possible, but OR.230 was beyond current means and should be left open. OR.229 was then vetted by the specialist research establishments of the Ministry of Supply and, having confirmed with the 'firms' that a practical airplane could be designed to meet the stipulation within the required time-scale, the Air Ministry then drew up a specification around it. Specification B.14/46 (re-issued as B.35/46) called for a medium-range jet-bomber for RAF use capable of carrying a 10,000lb bomb over a still-air range of 3,350 miles by day or night from any base in the world. It also had to be capable of carrying a wide range of conventional weapons and of being modified for reconnaissance duties, and 100,000lb was the maximum take-off weight because runways of the day were not long enough to get anything heavier airborne. However, on the advice of the aviation industry, this was later increased to 115,000lb.

The specification insisted on 45,000ft as the cruising altitude after one hour and 50,000ft two and a half hours after take-off. It was also hoped that the design would allow the bomber to exceed 50,000ft by as great a margin as possible, as weight reduced in direct relation to the fuel consumed. The cruising speed was to be 500kts (or Mach 0.875) at continuous power output over a target 1,500 miles from base. These figures, it was emphasised, were minimums, and it was hoped that they would be handsomely exceeded. The resulting specification B.35/46 called for a high degree of manoeuvrability and blind bombing capability using H2S radar.

Following the issue of B.35/46, on 24 January 1947 the major UK aircraft designers were invited to submit tenders; among them were Armstrong-Whitworth, Avro, Bristol, English Electric, Handley Page and Short Bros. Although these and other firms had been given a preliminary draft of B.35 options on 7 November 1946, a planned closing date for tenders of 5 March proved too optimistic and had to be extended to 30 April at the request of the industry.

Because of the revised specification and the changes in ideas and designs, the Air Ministry asked the Royal Aircraft Establishment at Farnborough to set up a project group of aerodynamicists and engineers under the Aerodynamic Flight Section with the remit of examining each designer's proposal and determining which one should be chosen.

Of the six formal tenders submitted in the closing month of May 1947, the most uncomplicated were those of the English Electric Co. and Vickers. English Electric's submission looked like a scaled-up Canberra, and the Vickers proposal incorporated the longest fuselage of all, supported by a high aspect ratio wing of about 26 degrees sweep. These two designs were quickly discounted on the grounds that they were not advanced enough for the needs envisaged post-1957.

This left Armstrong-Whitworth, Handley Page, Avro and Shorts, all with futuristic designs featuring pronounced swept-back wings, deltas, crescents and flying wings and so on – all advanced aeronautic designs. Avro and Handley Page were the only designs to feature four engines, Armstrong-Whitworth and Shorts both proposed five.

Eventually the Avro Co. was rated clear leader at the tender design conference of 28 July 1947, and a decision was reached to order the airplane designed under the leadership of the renowned Roy Chadwick and his team during early 1947 at Chadderton in Manchester. A.W. and H.P. were runners up and were both allowed to proceed to a wind-tunnel 'fly-off' as a means of providing a second design for a final, full-scale production back-up. This resulted on 15 January 1948 in the H.P. 80 design (later to be named Victor) being promoted to joint winner, while English Electric and Vickers were invited to compete in the production (in a shorter time-scale) of a slightly lower-technology 'insurance' airplane. Vickers won, and a separate specification B.9/48 was written round the V.660 design. In this way the RAF was given the Valiant two years before the first definitive Vulcan entered service, and it was the Valiant that dropped Britain's first A-bomb in 1956, and the first H-bomb (actually a higher-yield A-bomb) in 1957.

Acceptance of Vickers Valiant as the 'insurance' aircraft brought to an end Short Bros' involvement in the post-Second World War jet bomber programme, and the Short Sperrin (named after a range of mountains in Northern Ireland) of which two prototypes were built, was cancelled. However, the design of its pressure cabin paved the way for the same concept to be used on all the V-bombers.

Meanwhile, at Avro, problems were initially encountered with any designs put forward due to the limitation of the overall weight, but by changing the conventional airframe shape from a standard wing and tail to a delta shape it was found that the overall weight of the aircraft could be drastically reduced.

And so, by the spring of 1947, it was decided to proceed with the new delta-wing design, and the airplane that came to be known as the Avro Type 698 began to take shape.

An early delta-winged Avro Vulcan leads examples of the equally ambitious crescent, alterative-winged H.P. Victor and more conventional Vickers Valiant. All three were ordered into series production to meet one requirement. RAF chiefs were unable to decide between the Victor and the Vulcan, so both were ordered, while the somewhat simpler Vickers Valiant was ordered partly as insurance against failure of the two more radical designs and partly to provide Bomber Command with an early post-war long-range jet bomber to replace its ageing piston-engined Avro Lincoln aircraft that was based on the wartime Avro Lancaster. (*Take Off*, Part Works)

The Short S.A.4 Sperrin was designed to meet the Air Ministry's requirement for a low-cost interim heavy jet-bomber. The project suffered delays during ground testing, and was beaten into the air by the Vickers Valiant. Nonetheless, two prototypes were built and used for experimental and test work, including the dropping of dummy nuclear weapons. Though of conventional configuration – except for its four Avon jet engines positioned in vertical pairs above and below either wing – the Sperrin incorporated many advanced systems and performed valuable service in support of the V-bomber programme until the aircraft were eventually grounded as an economy measure. (*Take Off*, Part Works)

Vulcan B.2 touching down with air brakes extended and its massive brake parachute deployed. (Mike Hooks)

The pure delta prototype Type 698 VX770 (completed August 1952) bore the brunt of the early engine and other trials work along with the Avro 707 one-third-scale experimental aircraft, until it disintegrated in the air at RAF Syerston on 20 September 1958.

1 Avro Type 707A, serial WZ736, was made at Chadderton and assembled at Bracebridge Heath, in Lincolnshire. It made its maiden flight on 20 February 1953, when it flew from RAF Waddington to Avro Woodford. By this time the Avro Type 698 prototype VX770 had already flown and 'WZ736' was mainly used by the RAE to undertake test work not directly related to the Vulcan project. Many records associated with this work are held by the museum in Manchester's Library and Record Centre. WZ736 was retired in 1966, and was earmarked for display at the RAF Museum, Hendon, being allocated an instructional 'M' serial (7868M). It is believed it was also used as a source of spares to keep Avro 707C 'WZ744' flying. WZ736 was returned to Manchester in 1982, on loan from the RAF Museum. Following refurbishment by British Aerospace the aircraft was made available for display and in 2006 was still at the Greater Manchester Museum of Science & Industry in the north of England, where it has resided for many years. (Mike Hooks)

2 Avro Type 707C, serial WZ744, was built as a dual-seat crew familiarisation aircraft; it is now on display to the public at the Aerospace Museum, RAF Cosford, Shropshire. (Mike Hooks)

3 First production Vulcan B.1, serial XA889, completed in February 1955, seen here at the 1957 Farnborough Air Show, was a trials aircraft throughout its career until it was eventually scrapped in 1971. (Mike Hooks)

4 Vulcan B.2, serial XH536, completed in September 1959, served on trial duties and at RAF Waddington until it crashed in Wales on terrain following trials work on 11 February 1966. (Mike Hooks)

5 Vulcan B.2, serials XH537 and XH538, completed in August and September 1959 respectively, were both involved in Douglas Skybolt missile trials in the United States. Both aircraft served first with B Flight 230 OCU at RAF Finningley and then operationally with No.27 Squadron; XH537 was later used as an MRR airframe. XH538 also served with No.35 Squadron. XH537 was delivered to RAF Abingdon, Oxfordshire, on retirement in 1983. Vulcan XH538 was sold as scrap in 1981.

6 Vulcan B.2, serial XM655, completed in November 1964, served with Nos 9, 101, 44 and 50 Squadrons until its sale in February 1984. It was civil registered as G-VULC, later N655AV.

7 VX777 second Type 698 prototype, completed in September 1953, was used on trials and development work and came to be the B.2 prototype. It was eventually retired to Farnborough where it is seen lying derelict, minus its tail fin rudder, prior to scrapping in July 1963. (Mike Hooks)

8 *Opposite above:* Vulcan B.2 BS, serial XL388, was completed in June 1962 and served with No.9 Squadron, Nos 617 and 44 Squadrons and No.230 OCU, until its sale as scrap in 1985. (Mike Hooks)

9 *Opposite below:* Vulcan B.2 BB, serial XM598, completed in August 1963, served with Nos 9, 12, 44, 50 and 101 Squadrons and was selected for the Black Buck One mission in early 1982. However, it was forced to turn back unserviceable and took no further part in the operation. Almost immediately after the Falklands XM598 was retired to the Aerospace Museum at RAF Cosford, Shropshire, as serial 8778M. (Mike Hooks)

10 Vulcan B.2, serial XM606, completed in December 1963, served with Nos 12, 101 and 9 Squadrons until being presented to Barksdale AFB, USA, in June 1982. (Mike Hooks)

11 A camouflaged Vulcan B.2 BS on display with its under-fuselage Blue Steel missile clearly visible.

12 Vulcan B.2 BS showing bomb-bay 'slot' modification to permit recessed carriage of Blue Steel stand-off missile, giving rise to the B.2A designation. (Mike Hooks)

13 Vulcan B.2, serial XM595, completed in August 1963, was delivered to No.617 Squadron at RAF Scampton and was equipped to carry Blue Steel. XM595 also served with No.27 at the Lincolnshire base as part of the Scampton Bomber Wing, and No.35 Squadron at Coningsby. It was sold as scrap in 1982. (Mike Hooks)

14 Vulcan B.2, serial XM657, completed in January 1965, has the distinction of being the last B.2 built, and served with Nos 35, 101, 50 and 44 Squadrons respectively until it was scrapped.

15 English Electric Lightning supersonic air defence fighters with Red Top missiles operated with CENTO dedicated Avro Vulcan bombers from RAF Akrotiri, Cyprus. This example in No.74 'Tiger' Squadron markings, Lightning F.1A serial XM135, can be seen at the IWM Duxford, Cambridgeshire.

16 A superb view of distinctive re-roled low-level camouflaged conventional bombing Avro Vulcan B.2 climbing characteristically away on its steep ascent shortly after take-off from its UK base, with its undercarriage doors still to close. (J.S. Smith)

17 A camouflaged Avro Vulcan B.2 on approach at RNAS Yeovilton, in the West Country, in the early 1970s during one of that base's many 'Open Day' air shows. (Ron Smith)

18 With the RB 199 engine installation painted dark blue overall, XA903 is seen flying in the vicinity of the Severn Bridge that links England to Wales. (Mike Hooks)

19 XA903 in level flight follows the coastline of the West Country on another Turbo Union RB199 test flight. (Mike Hooks)

20 Camouflaged No.27 Squadron Avro Vulcan B.2 MRR on approach to land back at its Waddington, Lincolnshire, base following a routine operational reconnaissance patrol mission over the North Sea oil rigs and the east coast of England. (Ron Smith)

21 The ubiquitous Vulcan B.2, serial XH558, operated by No.27 Squadron, is seen here in MRR configuration and camouflage. Part of its work was to ensure the safety and security of the North Sea oil fields and oil rigs off the east coast of Scotland. (Mike Hooks)

22 Handley Page Victors were integral to the success of the Falklands campaign, not only as in-flight refuellers, but also in the reconnaissance role they took on during the earlier South Georgia operations. Here a Victor K2 tanker, serial XL231, is prepared for flight at its Marham, Norfolk, base in early 1982.

23 A sidewinder-equipped Fleet Air Arm BAe Sea Harrier FRS.1 is secured to the carrier deck en route the South Atlantic in early 1982.

24 Fitted with an in-flight refuelling probe and carrying self-defence sidewinder air-to-air missiles, the HS Nimrod MR.2 could patrol deep into the Arctic and Atlantic oceans from its base at RAF Kinloss in Scotland; but for Operation Corporate missions, Nimrods were airborne to act as search and rescue co-ordinators should the need arise, and on at least two occasions helped link the lone tanker and bomber, or assisted the bomber in the target area. Nimrods were forward-based at Ascension Island.

25 Post-Falklands, safely back in the UK, Vulcan B.2 BB, serial XM607, was proudly displayed in front of No.44 Squadron's hangar at Waddington on a number of occasions during base 'Open Days', sporting its three 'iron' bombs on its nose commemorating its three epic Black Buck missions flown in 1982.

26 Vulcan B.2 BB, serial XM607 (8779M), was completed in December 1963 and served with Nos 9, 35, 44, and 101 Squadrons. Veteran of three Falkland War Black Buck missions in 1982, it was withdrawn from use in January 1983 and has since been installed as Gate Guardian at RAF Waddington, Lincolnshire.

27 The EE Canberra was the first jet-powered bomber to enter RAF service. The prototype flew in May 1949 and production deliveries began two years later. Canberras were ordered in large numbers, and to meet demand Avro, Handley Page and Shorts became major sub-contractors, in order to series-produce the type. The design lent itself to considerable development and a number of variants were produced to undertake a variety of tasks, including photographic reconnaissance and night interdiction as well as bombing. It was first used operationally by the RAF during the 1956 Suez Crisis, when numerous missions were flown against Egyptian airfields and other military targets. This particular example, a B.6 serial XH568, has an extended nose radome which was specially built and fitted for radar trials with the then Royal Radar Establishment (RRE) at Malvern, where the aircraft was still resplendent in its 'Raspberry Ripple' livery. It has since been retired to Bruntingthorpe Aerodrome, Leicestershire, where former display Vulcan B.2 XH558 also resides.

28 Proudly sporting the Union Jack and City of Lincoln badge high on its tail, Vulcan B.2, serial XH558, taxies along Bruntingthorpe's perimeter track on its retirement to the Leicestershire Aerodrome in March 1993, where it has undergone major servicing before a possible return to flight in 2007.

Series Vulcan B.1 aircraft received the new 'kinked' Phase 2 wing leading edge; it was also retrofitted to the first sixteen B.1 aircraft of the original production batch which had been laid down with the 'pure' delta design. Aircraft towards the rear of the assembly hall appear to be fitted with the 'pure' delta. (Mike Hooks)

Sadly, Roy Chadwick, now Avro's Technical Director, would not see the results of his team's delta-wing work as he lost his life along with test pilot S.A. 'Bill' Thorn on 23 August 1947 at Avro's Woodford Aerodrome when taking off on an air-test following modifications to a sixty-passenger Avro Tudor 2 airliner prototype. Tragically, its aileron controls had been fitted the wrong way round.

While the delta design offered the major advantage of reducing the overall weight of the aircraft, it was not enough in itself to meet the required specification. Nevertheless, the design was persevered with and by using a standard circular-section fuselage ahead of the wing, thus merging it into a vast wing root, the bomber began to take shape.

The thickest part of the wing was swept sharply forward at the root until it appeared almost as a wedge at the fuselage. Although the overall appearance of the design seemed too thick at the leading edge, it was the only way to accommodate the large inlet ducts needed to ensure sufficient air reached the engines. The initial idea was to have the engines mounted in pairs, fed by circular intakes, although this was later revised to laying the engines side-by-side and having them fed from the 'letter-box' shaped intakes in the wings leading edge.

Another early idea, which was soon abandoned, was to put the 'special bomb' in the port wing and balance the weight with fuel in the starboard wing. However, it was found that by laying the engines in a row, the cross section of the wing could be reduced, and so the better solution was to put the bomb in a conventional centre-line compartment.

To assess both the H.P. 80 and the Avro Type 698 wing shapes, small-scale trials aircraft approximately one third the size of the bombers were built. However, the H.P. 88 crashed before any useful data could be obtained, and the four Avro 707s did not appear far enough in advance for any feedback to be incorporated in the prototype Vulcan's design. Often the 707A was being modified to reflect the changes in the full-sized airplane's design. The first of a total of five Avro 707s built suffered a fatal crash during September 1949, but four more were eventually constructed; these later aircraft incorporated ejector seats. The 707B did not fly until the autumn of 1950 and the high-speed 707A was still being built when the first Type 698 took to the air. In 1952, when the 707A had nearly caught up with its big brother by having power controls fitted, the first prototype Type 698, serial VX770, had already been assembled at the Woodford plant with sections sent over from Chadderton. It was at this time that it was discovered that the wing of the 707A 'buzzed' increasingly severely as height and speed increased, a fault soon to cause buffeting in the full-sized airplane, only to be cured by putting a 'kink' in the leading edges of the delta.

By then the Type 698 was in full production and sixteen leading edges had to be scrapped, an expensive set-back that could have been prevented had the 707 programme (which was supposed to prevent this) been properly co-ordinated and timed. Nevertheless, the 707A and 707B airplanes did prove the delta-wing design worked and, without them, the Avro Type 698 might have proved an unacceptable risk. The Avro 707C was designed as a two-seat crew familiarisation trainer, but spent most of its life on powered control development work.

A mock-up of the new 'kinked' Phase 2 wing leading edge was tested successfully on the Avro 707A in 1954, and also on VX777 (the second prototype Type 698) on 5 October 1955. This meant that the special envelope jigging for the leading edge had to be completely rebuilt and the sixteen leading edges of the aircraft in production would need fitting with the new design. It also marked the end of the pure delta-shaped wing.

2

Trials and Development

Apart from the five one-third-size Avro 707s, in total thirty-two Avro Vulcans were involved at various times in both the trials and the development programmes, some to such an extent that they were never deployed operationally. In addition to the two Type 698 prototypes, VX770 and VX777, the following series production aircraft were involved:

Serial	Date completed	Remarks
VX770	Aug. 1952	disintegrated during a Battle of Britain air display at RAF Syerston on 20 Sep. 1958.
VX777	Sep. 1953	became prototype B.2 then retired to Farnborough – scrapped in Jul. 1963
XA889 B.1	Feb. 1955	scrapped in 1971
XA890 B.1	1955	scrapped in 1971
XA891 B.1	1955	crashed near Hull on 24 Jul. 1959
XA892 B.1	1955	also used on ground instructional duties until scrapped in 1972
XA893 B.1	1956	scrapped in 1962 – cockpit section at RAF Museum, Cosford (8591M)
XA894 B.1	1957	destroyed at Patchway (ground fire) on 3 Dec. 1962
XA895 B.1A	Aug. 1956	230 OCU/trials until it was sold as scrap, Sep. 1968
XA896 B.1	Mar. 1957	230 OCU/83/44/trials until it was scrapped, 1966
XA897 B.1	Jul. 1956	230 OCU/trials – crashed at London Heathrow Airport, 1 Oct. 1956
XA898 B.1	Jan. 1957	also used on ground instructional duties until it was scrapped in 1971
XA899 B.1	Feb. 1957	also used on ground instructional duties until it was scrapped in 1973
XA900 B.1	Mar. 1957	230 OCU/101 then ground instructional duties – scrapped in 1986
XA901 B.1	Apr. 1957	230 OCU/44/83 then ground instructional duties – scrapped in 1972

XA902 B.1	May 1957	230 OCU/engine trials – R-R Spey turbofans, eventually destined to power the American MDC F-4K Phantom II, were ordered for the FAA and RAF in preference to the GE J79 turbojets fitted to US air arms aircraft. XA902 was damaged during landing in Feb. 1958 and was subsequently scrapped in 1963
XA903 B.1	May 1957	Blue Steel 100/Bristol Olympus 593 Concorde engine and R-R/Turbo-Union RB.199 for the Tornado aircraft – scrapped in 1980
XH478 B.1A	Mar. 1958	83/44/trials then ground instructional duties until it was scrapped
XH499 B.1A	Jul. 1958	617/50/44/trials until being scrapped
XH533 B.2	Aug. 1958	sold as scrap – 1970
XH534 B.2 MRR	Jul. 1959	trials/27 until sold as scrap in 1982
XH535 B.2	May 1960	crashed near Andover, Hampshire, 11 May 1964
XH536 B.2	Jul. 1959	trials/Waddington – crashed in Wales (terrain-following radar trial) 11 Feb. 1966
XH537 B.2 MRR	Aug. 1959	trials/230/27 – to RAF Abingdon 1983. cockpit section now at Bruntingthorpe Aerodrome, Leicestershire (8749M)
XH538 B.2	Sep. 1959	trials/230/27/35 until it was sold as scrap in 1981
XH539 B.2	Sep. 1959	trials then ground instructional duties until being scrapped
XH555 B.2	Jun. 1961	27/230/trials until scrapping in 1971
XH557 B.2	May 1960	trials/RAF Cottesmore/Waddington/Akrotiri – scrapped in 1982
XJ784 B.2	Mar. 1961	trials/230/9/44/101 until it was sold as scrap in 1982
XL317 B.2 BS	Jul. 1961	trials/617/230 OCU – scrapped
XL391 B.2 BB	May 1963	trials/9/101/44 – sold in Feb. 1983
XM596	not completed	fatigue tests – scrapped in 1972
XM603 B.2	Nov. 1963	9/50/101/44 – sold to BAe in Mar. 1982, mock-up for K.2 mods
XM612 B.2 BB	Feb. 1964	9/101/44/trials – sent to Norwich Museum in Jan. 1983

Flown for the first time on 30 August 1952, VX770 obviously bore the brunt of early development work in particular this involved trials associated with the new Rolls-Royce Conway engines.

Initially fitted with four Rolls-Royce Avon turbojets of 48.9kN (11,000lb) thrust, these were later replaced with Armstrong Siddeley Sapphire 6s before test R-R Conways were fitted. The Mk.5 Conways fitted at Langar, Nottinghamshire, were rated at 67.2kN (15,000lb) thrust.

Flight trials of the Conway engines fitted to VX770 were flown from the Rolls-Royce airfield at Hucknall, near Derby, in the summer of 1958 under the supervision of R-R chief test pilot Jim Heyworth. The aircraft was flown by a mixture of civilian crews and a newly 'qualified' crew from 230 OCU, which had been the first to join the reformed No.617 Squadron at RAF Scampton.

An early Vulcan B.1 in EMI test rig was used to assess the effects of electromagnetic interference on aircraft and equipment.

Vulcan B.1, serial XA895, of the first production batch was completed in August 1956 with the original all-silver scheme and a black radome and fin tip. After service with No.230 OCU and as a trials aircraft, XA895 was sold as scrap in September 1968. (*Take Off*, Part Works)

Vulcan B.1, serial XA902, was completed in May 1957 and initially delivered to No.230 OCU at Waddington. It was made available to Rolls-Royce at Hucknall for engine trials. It is seen here touching down at Hucknall following an air test; damaged during landing in February 1958 it was scrapped in 1963. (Mike Hooks)

Vulcan B.1, serial XA899, was completed in February 1957 and did not see operational service as it was used throughout its career as a trial and ground instructional aircraft (serial 7812M). XA899 was scrapped in 1973. (Mike Hooks)

Vulcan B.2, serial XH539, completed in September 1959, served all its career as an trials and instructional airframe until scrapped. It is depicted carrying recessed under fuselage Blue Steel missile accompanied by three supersonic EE Lightning Mk.lA air defence fighters.

Bristol Olympus Mk.201 engines developing 75.6kN (17,000lb) thrust were tested and developed in the second prototype VX777, having first flown fitted to the aircraft in September 1953. (Mike Hooks)

At the same time as the definitive Bristol Olympus Mk.201 engines developing 75.6kN (17,000lb) thrust were being fitted to series production aircraft, they were also being tested and developed in the second prototype VX777, having first flown fitted to the aircraft in September 1953.

But, in 1957, with the previous British Government's enforced rationalisation of the aviation industry in Britain in full swing, the Ministry of Supply decided that Britain needed only one big jet engine and chose the R-R Conway. Support for the Bristol Olympus was withdrawn and Avro were instructed to redesign the Vulcan to take the Conway. This they were reluctant to do, as the decision had been made on purely financial grounds rather than an in-depth assessment of the technical aspects of the two engines. At this point, Bristol Aero Engines offered to develop the Olympus 200 Series at their own expense and this unexpected generosity saved it from extinction. In the event, it was developed more cheaply than had been expected and, as we now know, was brilliantly successful. The company subsequently produced the 300 Series engines with upwards of 88.9kN (20,000lb) of static thrust and, in conjunction with SNECMA, a much developed derivative to power the Aérospatiale/BAC Concorde SST.

Unlike the Vulcan B.1s delivered to the RAF which were well equipped with navigational aids: (including Green Satin – a Doppler product which fed into a ground position indicator, a Navigation/Bombing System (NBS), a radio compass, and in later years TACAN (TACtical Aid to Navigation) and a periscope sextant for visual plotting by way of the stars), VX770 was instead packed with test equipment, cameras and instruments, and only one radio compass for navigation.

As the Conway engine trials work continued at Hucknall throughout the summer, VX770 was shown off to the public at several air shows, but only when it didn't interfere with planned air tests. On 1 and 6 September it was demonstrated at the Farnborough Show.

A few days later, on 20 September, flown by an all-civilian crew, with the exception of the navigator/plotter RAF Flt Lt 'Polly' Parrot, VX770 disintegrated in front of spectators at the RAF Syerston Battle of Britain Day display. The crew were killed.

Many articles were written in the aviation press 'explaining' the accident. One in *Air Clues* suggested the most plausible explanation was that:

> The engines (R-R Conways) were so much more powerful than the ones previously fitted that during the low-level high-speed flypast, the design limit was exceeded. The wing leading edge skin started to 'peel' back, exposing the internal structure to the full force of the airflow and the whole wing just came apart.

The article concluded this was not a fatigue failure, but it did serve as a potent reminder that the safety factors built into aircraft structures are very marginal, and the 'never exceed' limits should always be strictly observed.

One of the many lessons learnt from this horrendous accident was that not only was it undesirable to fly the Vulcan at low-level and high-speed for safety reasons, it was unnecessary from the spectators' point of view as the airplane was a big, majestic, powerful, noisy and manoeuvrable beast near the ground and did not need speed to show it off. That was better left to the smaller combat aircraft.

Another early Vulcan that also participated in both the company's engine trials and much of the other trial and development work, including Blue Steel 100A, was XA903. When the aircraft left Avro Woodford on 31 May 1957 it was the fifteenth production airplane and only the third Vulcan to be finished in anti-flash white; it joined the test fleet at A&AEE Boscombe Down, Wiltshire, that day. From there it took part in the early stages of the Blue Steel missile programme and flew at Farnborough with a dummy fitted.

Vulcan B.1, serial XA903, was completed in May 1957 and joined the test fleet at A&AEE Boscombe Down, Wiltshire, on 31 May. From here it took part in the initial Blue Steel missile programme work. It is seen here flying at Farnborough with a dummy missile. (Mike Hooks)

Nevertheless, XA903 spent almost all its career as an engine flying test-bed for Bristol Siddeley. The engines under test slung under the bomb-bay on the aircraft's centre-line. (Mike Hooks)

Initially engine test flying involved many hours with a development Bristol – SNECMA Olympus 593, intended to power the Aerospatiale/BAC Concorde SST. Here XA903 is seen with a slatted louvered door lowered ahead of the test engine's air inlet. The somewhat unusual external electrical cabling can be seen running from the bomb-bay to the improvised engine inlet assembly. (Mike Hooks)

Serial XA903, minus the adjustable louvered door assembly, on approach to Bristol Siddeley, Filton, after completing another Aerospatiale/BAC Olympus 593 engine test flight. (Mike Hooks)

On completion of Olympus 593 testing, XA903 was converted to undertake a flying test programme for the Turbo Union RB 199 engine intended for the Panavia Tornado multi-role combat aircraft, with test flying expected to total some 320 hours. (Mike Hooks)

Vulcan B.2, serial XH534, was completed in July 1959 and served as an ECM trials aircraft until its conversion to B.2 (MRR) standard when delivered to No.27 Squadron at Waddington, where it remained until it was sold as scrap in 1982. (Mike Hooks)

Vulcan B.2, serial XH539, completed in September 1959, spent all of its flying career on trials work and ground instructional duties until being scrapped. Note low-visibility toned-down national markings. (Mike Hooks)

In 1964 it was flown to Rolls-Royce at Filton, Bristol, for modifications to allow the aircraft to test the Bristol Siddeley Olympus 593 engine under development for the Anglo-French Concorde SST. After two years of extensive modification work, the aircraft flew again on 9 September 1966 and was used for icing trials (among others), with the Concorde power plant slung underneath the fuselage.

On completion of these trials in 1971, XA903 was flown to Marshalls of Cambridge for yet more conversion work. This time it was to be fitted with an R-R/Turbo Union RB-199-34R engine, under development for use in the Panavia Tornado multi-role combat aircraft that was to replace the Vulcan. It was also fitted with a 27mm Mauser cannon (also fitted to the Tornado) – the first and only time such a weapon was fitted to a Vulcan. The aircraft flew again on 19 April 1973 and spent the next five years on engine and cannon trials on behalf of the Tornado programme. Upon completion of this programme in August 1978, XA903 had flown 125 test flights with different variants of the RB.199 slung underneath its fuselage. It entered the aviation history books as the last B.1 Vulcan to fly and eventually flew into retirement at RAE Farnborough, Hampshire, on 22 February 1979.

Here, after completing antenna-fitting static tests, it was used for fire-fighting and rescue training, and by 1984 when sold for scrap was looking much the worse for wear. Even so, by then the nose section had been removed and purchased by the Wales Museum at Cardiff-Wales Airport, south Glamorgan. Here it remained until 1992 when it passed into private ownership for a mere £400!

3

Taking Flight

Construction of the first Type 698 prototype began in 1951 during the time Avro was running the third-scale Type 707 aircraft programme. The 698 airframe was built at Chadderton, although the delta wings were constructed at Woodford.

In June 1952 Avro were informed that twenty-five Type 698 production aircraft and twenty-five H.P. 80s were to be ordered for the RAF, as both types had their strengths and weaknesses and these initial airplanes would enable squadron-level assessment of both types to be undertaken. In the event, the RAF could not choose between the pair, and both designs were to be ordered in parallel for some time to come.

Various names for the two designs were proposed but it was the Chief of the Air Staff, Sir John Slessor, who later in the year decided that the Type 698 and H.P. 80 designs would adopt names beginning with the letter 'V' (to follow the already established Vickers Valiant) and so Avro's 698 became the Vulcan and the H.P. 80 became the Victor.

So, the Vulcan was born, as was the V-Force (as it later became known), both of which were destined to take their place in the annals of Britain's military aviation history.

Flown by Wing Commander 'Roly' Falk, the first all-white prototype Type 698, serial VX770, was an impressive sight as it took to the air for its maiden flight from Woodford on 30 August 1952. Hastened through the ground running and taxiing trials, this aircraft at the time still had no second pilot's seat, cockpit pressurisation or wing fuel system.

Although it was originally intended that the aircraft be powered by Bristol BE.10 turbojets (later designated Olympus), these were not completed in time and so VX770 flew on four R-R Avon R.A.3s. The Avons produced only 6,500lb of thrust per engine and the following year the aircraft was re-engined with Armstrong Siddeley Sapphires capable of 7,500lb thrust.

A mere two days after its first flight, VX770 was flown to Boscombe Down and, after clocking up only three hours' flying time, it was bringing forth gasps of wonder from the crowds gathered at the 1952 Farnborough Air Show. The aviation press waxed lyrical and filled their pages with column upon column of reports on the prototype bomber's five public appearances, when on each occasion Roly Falk showed off the vast white delta to its best advantage, culminating on the final day in a neat 'Vic' formation with the blue Avro 707B on one wing and the red 707A on the other.

Flight magazine subsequently devoted a whole article to the question of what to call the new bomber, coming up with all manner of contrived appendages to Avro until it settled on the Avro 'Albion'. The staff of this otherwise responsible publication were obviously blissfully unaware that the job had already been done for them by CAS Sir John Slessor.

Another view of the resplendent first prototype Type 698 VX770, first flown from Avro Woodford on 30 August 1952 by Avro's chief test pilot, 'Roly' Falk.

First Vulcan prototype Type 698, serial VX770, completed in August 1952 at Avro Woodford, was displayed at that year's Farnborough Air Show, Hampshire, in the south of England, by Wing Commander 'Roly' Falk, despite the fact that the aircraft had not been fully fitted out. (Ron Smith)

Following Farnborough, VX770 was grounded pending modification of the undercarriage fairings (which had fallen off on the first flight), and the installation of all the remaining items including the co-pilot's seat. Roly Falk designed the Vulcan cockpit personally, and he decided that, as it was so easy to fly, instead of the bomber's conventional spectacle control column it should have a fighter-type stick to get away from the Second World War heavy-bomber design.

Because Falk had flown the airplane solo at Farnborough, and because the flight deck of production aircraft had their twin ejection seats arrayed so close together that they resembled a sardine can, the myth was that the Vulcan cockpit was originally designed for one pilot and the second seat was crushed in only as an afterthought by the RAF. This is untrue, as two-pilot operation was written into the original specification. Falk actually argued that one man could fly a Vulcan and he couldn't understand what the other man was there for, but the RAF reminded him that the days of letting a newly qualified pilot loose on an expensive front-line bomber, as they had done with the wartime Halifaxes and Lancasters, were over, and they needed the co-pilot's seat to train the captains of the future, and to cope if the first pilot was incapacitated in any way.

The front fuselage forward of the wing roots consisted primarily of a pressure cabin for the crew of five. Pilot and co-pilot sat high up on Martin-Baker ejection seats under a large jettisonable blister canopy which was totally opaque apart from the windscreen and a circular window on each side. As with all V-bombers, little provision was made for all-round vision, the theory being that the structural weaknesses inherent in incorporating windscreens should be kept to a minimum, especially as the bomber was to operate almost continuously at altitudes around 50,000ft. Nor was it deemed necessary for the crew to have good all-round vision for defensive purposes when contemporary fighters and interceptors were unable to operate at these altitudes, so the pilots were left to view their surroundings en route to the target in what amounted to a letter-box with bars.

The second prototype, serial VX777, differed from the first in several ways. It was powered by Bristol Olympus Mk.100 engines, capable of 9,750lb thrust, and incorporated a specific crew compartment. The fuselage was made slightly longer to increase internal fuel capacity and accommodate a longer nose-wheel leg.

This prototype went a long way to meeting the specification, particularly with the design of the crew compartment. VX777 first flew on 3 September 1953.

The programme suffered a set-back in July 1954 when VX777 suffered a heavy landing at Farnborough which promptly grounded the airplane for several months. This slowed the development programme, particularly the high-speed and high-altitude trials, although other trial work continued using VX770. Still, two prototypes were in any case inadequate for the amount of trials work needed before the type could enter service, leaving much to be done by the early production aircraft.

Fortunately, VX777 resumed trials in 1955, by which time the first series production B.1 was virtually complete. The new leading edge arrived too late to be fitted on the first production aircraft, serial XA889, which was rolled out at Woodford in January 1955. Painted overall silver and featuring a new nose-cone, XA889 was fitted initially with Olympus 100 engines and made its maiden flight on 4 February 1955. Also in 1955, to demonstrate the Vulcan's fine handling qualities, strength and amazing power, Avro's chief test pilot 'Roly' Falk, in an unprecedented manoeuvre, rolled B.1 XA890 on the first trade day of the 1955 Farnborough Air Show to the complete astonishment of those present, including prominent members of the aviation press and many aviation company business executives.

Pure delta all-over white second prototype Vulcan Type 698, serial VX777, on approach at Farnborough's main runway. Shortly after this photograph was taken, VX777 suffered a heavy landing at RAE Farnborough which promptly grounded the aircraft for several months. (Ron Smith)

Avro Vulcan bombers soon became a common sight over Lincolnshire from 1957 onwards. Of the five aircraft on dispersal, three white-painted B.1s added to No.83 Squadron's strength, and the two all-over silver aircraft in the background were part of No.230 OCU.

With powerful 11,000lb thrust Mk.101 engines fitted, XA889 was delivered to Boscombe Down for service acceptance trials in March/April 1956; the initial Certificate of Airworthiness release came on 29 May and the RAF received its first Vulcan XA897 (the ninth production aircraft) on 20 July. This airplane was temporarily attached to No.230 Operational Conversion Unit (OCU) at RAF Waddington, Lincolnshire, but in August it accompanied XA895 to Boscombe Down, where each aircraft flew 20–30 hours a week on Operational Reliability Trials. XA897 then returned to Avro Woodford for modifications prior to setting out from Boscombe on 9 September on a 'shop window' flight. This was Operation Tasman, a flight to New Zealand via the Air Force Commemoration Week in Melbourne – the venue of the Olympic Games that year.

The aircraft was flown by Squadron Leader Donald 'Podge' Howard DFC with his co-pilot Air Marshal Sir Harry Broadhurst (the C-in-C of Bomber Command). Three Squadron Leaders, Albert Gamble (Wireless and Electronics Officer), Edward Eames, AFC (Navigator) and James Stroud (Radar Navigator and qualified Vulcan pilot) were all specially chosen for their skill and experience. They sat in the rear seats, along with Avro technical services representative Frederick Bassett, who occupied the cabin-well seat, as the company's representative on this long-range proving flight. The bomber arrived in Christchurch on 18 September 1956 in a flight time of twenty-three hours, nine minutes, having transited via Aden, Singapore, and Melbourne, Australia.

Soon after, XA897 left New Zealand for its return trip to the UK; after covering more than 26,000 miles it was planned that it would arrive back at Heathrow to a VIP reception on 1 October having journeyed to Aden via Brisbane, Darwin, Singapore and Ceylon. At 2.50 a.m. (local time) on the morning of 1 October, XA897 took off from RAF Khormaksar, Aden, in the clear night sky on the final leg of its round trip. The crew were told that the weather forecast for the afternoon of 1 October at London Heathrow was rain with poor visibility and a low cloud base, but there was high-intensity lighting and normal airline traffic, so no difficulty was anticipated.

Squadron Leader Howard, as aircraft captain, elected to carry out a ground-controlled approach (GCA) to land at Heathrow with the option of diverting to RAF Waddington where the weather was decidedly better.

However, by the time XA897 was aligned at 6 miles out on the centre-line of runway 10 Left for a GCA, the sky had become very overcast, the cloud extremely low, and surface visibility was down to 500ft in what was at times torrential rain.

What followed was a most tragic event, in full view of the host of spectators awaiting the aircrafts historic set-down. Instead of a triumphant and safe landing, they were to witness through the murk the huge bomber, still 2,000ft short of the runway; climbing away from the ground at full power with the landing gear extended. The two pilots were then seen to eject before the large delta-winged aircraft rolled right and crashed into the ground, killing the four rear crew compartment members.

From the inevitable subsequent inquiry, both pilots and the ground-controller gave evidence to the accident investigation board. It was stated that the talk-down appeared normal until the aircraft struck a ditch short of, and offset from, the runway.

In the final seconds before the impact, the crew had realised they were dangerously low and Howard elected to overshoot, at which point the aircraft clipped the ground, 'tearing off' the main undercarriage – parts of which hit the wing. Accelerating and climbing, at about 250ft the nose and starboard wing dropped and the big bomber began to roll to the right and, unable to control the aircraft anymore, Howard and Broadhurst ejected, leaving it to crash into the ground with the loss of the rear crew who had no chance of escaping their fate.

Left: Though deliveries of series Vulcan B.1 began to increase, No.83 Squadron Vulcan B.1 on dispersal at Waddington in late 1957 still includes serial XA900 and one other from 230 OCU, as well as XA905, XA906 and one other anti-flash, white-finished squadron aircraft.

Below: Three early No.83 Squadron Vulcan B.1 in anti-flash white, the serials XA907, XA905 and one other XA are seen here airborne over the English countryside. (Mike Hooks)

Numerous investigations and theories failed to provide a definitive answer as to the cause of the accident. The aircraft suffered no technical malfunction although errors in the altimeters were found to be a contributory cause. In addition, it was determined that Howard had descended below his planned decision-altitude, at which point an overshoot should have been initiated; however, not enough ground proximity warning was given by the ground-controller to the bomber's pilot. With Howard and Broadhurst lucky to survive, and four valuable colleagues lost, the question has often been asked, would the accident have happened if Bomber Command HQ (who were fully aware of the predicted weather conditions in the London area at the planned touch-down time), had not signalled Aden saying XA897 should make a VIP landing at London Airport? It is thought that with sufficient fuel remaining, Howard, in all probability, would have opted to land at RAF Waddington, though he was never to admit to this. In the end, following a special investigation of the incident by the Ministry of Supply, it was concluded that the accident was a classic case of a whole series of small errors, omissions and events that ultimately were to lead to a major disaster.

By the end of 1956 seven production B.1s had been delivered, although the loss of XA897 meant only six remained (XA889-893 and XA895). All these airplanes, except XA895, were devoted entirely to trials work. By the beginning of 1957 the production Vulcans were also available for delivery to No.230 OCU at RAF Waddington, Lincolnshire, on a permanent basis, and were therefore ready for RAF front-line service. By the end of 1958 there were Vulcan squadrons at RAF Waddington, Finningley and Scampton. The second B.1 delivered to 230 OCU was XA898 on 3 January 1957, and crew conversion commenced in February that year. During the next few months, three more aircraft arrived (XA900, XA901 and XA902), during which time the all-over aluminium finish the first Vulcans were delivered in had made way for the anti-flash white paint scheme. The OCU operated Vulcan B.1s until June 1960.

By now, more than six years had passed since the original specification had been issued and Avro invited to tender. The Type 698 programme had not been without set-backs, and at times it must have seemed to Avro impossible, or at least unlikely, that it would ever meet the expectations placed upon it.

However, the results of six years of hard work by the design, development and production teams were about to reach fruition, with No.83 Squadron at RAF Waddington set to receive its first operational aircraft on 11 July 1957.

The first Vulcan crews of 230 OCU No.1 Course completed their training on 21 May 1957, and on the same day the RAF formed its first Vulcan squadron, No.83, to be co-located at RAF Waddington, even though their four Vulcan B.1 aircraft were only on loan from the OCU.

Having disbanded at Hemswell on 1 January 1956, the Vulcan was the squadron's first (and only) jet aircraft in its history. Unlike other Bomber Command squadrons which had seen service with the RAF's first jet bomber, the E.E. Canberra, No.83 Squadron had operated the piston-engined Avro Lincoln B.2 since 1946.

Crews completing the second course also went straight to No.83 Squadron, while the crews from the next course were allocated to No.101 Squadron to reform at RAF Finningley on 15 October 1957.

No.101 Squadron had been the first RAF squadron to operate a jet bomber when it took delivery of the first E.E. Canberra B.2s at RAF Binbrook in May 1951 and by December 1957 the last of the original twenty-five series production Avro Vulcan aircraft ordered in August 1952 (XA889–XA913) had been delivered.

A second order for thirty-seven airplanes had been placed in September 1954, and by the formation of the third Vulcan squadron (No.617 'Dambusters' at RAF Scampton on 1 May

1958), the first seven of this second batch of B.1 (XH475–XH481) had been completed. As one of the most famous RAF squadrons of all, 'The Dambusters' had disbanded at the end of 1955 having been based at RAF Binbrook, Lincolnshire, since 1946. The squadron had been the second bomber unit to receive the E.E. Canberra in January 1952 and so already had experience of the operation of the new jet-age bomber aircraft.

The squadron's reformation at RAF Scampton was particularly poignant as No.617 was returning home to the site of its 1943 formation, a location which had also served as the training base for the famous attack on the Rhur Dams. The first of the Vulcan B.1 units, XH482, was delivered on 5 May 1958, closely followed by serials XH483 and XH497. All three aircraft were completed in May that year and were later modified to B.1A standard.

The entry into squadron service of the Vulcan was, sadly, further marred by the loss of No.83 Squadron's serial XA908 in America on 24 October 1958 when the aircraft was on a 'Lone Ranger' training exercise flying from Goose Bay, Labrador, to Lincoln, AFB, Nebraska. The aircraft crashed 60 miles north-east of Detroit, Michigan, following an electrical failure with the loss of the entire crew. Until this accident it was believed that in the event of a DC electrical power failure, the reserve battery on board the airplane (the size of a small sofa) would provide twenty minutes' worth of standby power to keep the plane flying. But after only three minutes the crew of XA908 found to their horror that the emergency battery was exhausted.

This led to a modification to the Vulcan fleet to ensure the same tragedy did not occur again. But XA891 had not been modified in time and suffered the same failure during a trial flight from Woodford on 24 July 1959 which resulted in the loss of the aircraft, although this time the crew survived.

Despite these losses, the entering into service of the new delta-winged bomber had appeared to go well and seemed to offer great promise for the future. It was hoped that the Vulcan would assume the mantle of Britain's premier nuclear deterrent, the status that had been the sole preserve since July 1955 of the less sophisticated Vickers Valiant. No.83 Squadron then embarked on a series of goodwill flights, three Vulcan B.1s going to Africa for visits to Uganda, Kenya and Southern Rhodesia in March 1958 followed by two aircraft, one carrying AVM 'Gus' Walker, that travelled to Argentina and Brazil. Later in the same year AVM Walker was aboard a Vulcan which went eastwards via Turkey to the Philippines; the plane was also demonstrated to the RAAF at their base in Butterworth, Malaya. No.101 Squadron was soon also deployed on goodwill visits, two Vulcans deploying to Vietnam in November 1958.

Having seen the Vulcan through its early, and unusually difficult, 'teething-stage', not uncommon with the entry of a new military aircraft into service, it was time to further develop the design with even greater capabilities in mind. It was, after all, a long-range strategic nuclear bomber, and, therefore, had to be prepared and equipped, if necessary, to go to war.

Meanwhile, two crews from 230 OCU underwent extensive training for the annual Bomber Command competition and, in June 1957, flying against experienced Vickers Valiant crews, they won four of the six trophies up for grabs. This led AVM G.A. (Gus) Walker, AOC No.1 Group, to ask Bomber Command to enter the Valiant and Vulcan crews in the prestigious USAF SAC Bombing, Navigation and Reconnaissance competition that year. Both flew to America to participate in Operation Longshot; the code-name proved to be extremely apt, as the Vulcan crews came nowhere and the Valiants of No.3 Group did only slightly better, placing twenty-seventh out of the forty-five teams competing. Subsequently, formation of the Giant Voice Flight to specifically train Vulcan B.2 crews for the competition brought better results, with the competition subsequently won outright on at least two occasions.

Many overseas Vulcan B.1 'goodwill' flights were supported by Vickers Valiant BK.1 in-flight refuelling tankers drawn from No.214 Squadron, based at RAF Marham, Norfolk. (Mike Hooks)

Vulcan B.1, serial XH479, completed in March 1958 in the second production batch, was re-designated B.1A as a result of receiving an ECM suite in the re-designed tail fairing. Thirty B.1 aircraft received this modification between October 1960 and March 1963. XH479 served with Nos 44 and 83 Squadrons, then as an instrumentation aircraft until its withdrawal from use around 1967/68. It was subsequently re-registered as a ground instructional airframe serial 7974M at the RAF apprentice training school at RAF Halton, Buckinghamshire. The airframe was scrapped in 1973. A Hunting Percival Pembroke P.66 light eight-seat communications aircraft can also be seen; the aircraft is on static display at a Halton open-day. (Mike Hooks)

Vulcan B.1, serial XH497, with Phase 2 wing, completed in May 1958, served with No.617 'Dambusters' Squadron (later modified to B.1A standard with ECM pod) and No.50 Squadron until it was scrapped in 1969. (*Take Off*, Part Works)

By April 1959 a total of forty-five Vulcan B.1s had been delivered. But it soon became clear to RAF 'top brass', as the aircraft prepared to enter a new decade, that it would need to be modified to meet the ever-changing threat from the Soviet Union, particularly considering the change in Soviet fighter tactics.

It had been intended to fit electronic countermeasures systems into the B.2 airframes but, rather than wait, it was decided to modify thirty of the B.1 fleet to B.1A standard, thus providing each aircraft with its own self-contained warning and jamming suite, permitting greater autonomy. This involved re-designing the rear fuselage to accommodate the equipment which included a tail warning radar and aerial installation. Conversion was achieved between October 1960 and March 1963. Tail-cones were enlarged to include the rearward-looking radar, code-named Red Steer, and a chaff-dispenser chute, whilst a flat-plate aerial was added between the two starboard jet-pipes to connect with the Blue Diver jamming equipment.

The first B.1A production conversion was completed by Armstrong-Whitworth in August 1960, whereupon XH505 was redelivered to No.617 Squadron, but although the B.1A incorporated the Mk.2 jamming kit and modified tail, it was impossible to modify the whole electrical system from DC to AC to supply the new equipment, so instead the ECM equipment had to be supplied from an additional engine-driven alternator similar to that incorporated in the No.18 Squadron ECM Vickers Valiants.

4

Avro Vulcan B.2 and Vulcan Wing/Squadron Markings

Eight additional B.1s had been ordered on 31 March 1955 but by then Bristol Siddeley were already talking about an Olympus engine capable of developing 20,000lb of static thrust. To take full advantage of the higher operating-altitudes such engines would permit, Roy Ewans, Avro's chief designer after July 1955, knew he would have to re-design the whole outer Vulcan wing in order to increase still further the lift and margin for manoeuvre at altitude. Carrying on where the Phase 2 wing left off, Ewans' team designed the Phase 2C wing with an increased span of some 12ft, and with a far greater area. The more efficient use of the greater power also extended the bombers radius of action by 250 to 300 miles.

These new wings and engines were to form the basis of the Vulcan B.2, twenty-four series production models which were ordered on 25 February 1956. Trials of the new wing in flight were a great success, with Vulcan XH533 reaching 61,500ft on 4 March 1959, and nothing vindicated the Phase 2C assembly more forcibly than the following entry under 'Airframe Limitations' in the Vulcan crew manual: 'There is no height restriction on the aircraft because of airframe limitations'.

It was now necessary to get the new production variant into squadron service as soon as possible, and so seventeen aircraft originally destined to be B.1 variants were switched to the new B.2 standard early in the construction stage. As part of the B.2 development programme, a number of Vulcan B.1 trials aircraft were modified to carry out various B.2 trials:

XA890 avionics trials
XA891 fitted with Olympus 200 engines
XA892 weapons research
XA893 electrical system development
XA894 new ECM suite development
XA899 avionics research

To emphasise the urgency of the new variant, the first production B.2 (XH533) made its first flight on 19 August 1958 – six months before the last B.1 (XH532) flew. The second production B.2 (XH534) was the first Vulcan powered by uprated Olympus 201 engines of 17,000lb thrust, and by 1960 the 201s were being fitted to all production B.2s.

The first seven production B.2s (XH533–539) were used as trials aircraft and never received the full improvements made to the later series aircraft for the operational squadrons.

Above: No.83 Squadron was the first to receive Vulcan B.2s, delivered in anti-nuclear flash 'tone-down' finish, among them serial No.XH563, completed in December 1960. XH563 served with Nos 83 and 12 Squadrons, 230 OCU and latterly with No.27 Squadron in MRR configuration, until its scrapping.

Left: Nine Vulcan B.2s line-up at RAF Scampton for Exercise 'Mayflight' during May 1961. (*Lincolnshire Echo*)

On 1 July 1960 the first B.2 (XH558) was delivered to the No.230 OCU at RAF Waddington, followed by four more (XH559–562) before the end of the year.

As with the introduction of the B.1 aircraft into operational service in 1956, the first crews to carry out training on the B.2 were posted to a new No.83 Squadron established at RAF Scampton at the end of the course in December 1960, with the Waddington contingent reduced to a cadre of B.1s in August 1960 and re-numbered No.44 Squadron. The squadron received its first B.1A in January 1961. In June 1961 No.44 Squadron was joined by No.101 Squadron, which moved its aircraft over to Waddington from Finningley, while No.230 OCU moved the other way. On moving to Finningley the OCU split into two flights – 'A' Flight for Vulcan B.1 and B.1A training and 'B' Flight for B.2 training.

Finally, No.50 Squadron became the last B.1/B.1A unit to reform on 1 August 1961 with aircraft received from No.617 Squadron. This exercise served to concentrate all the B.1 and B.1A aircraft at Waddington.

By April 1961 No.83 Squadron had received a total of six aircraft and the build-up of the B.2 fleet continued with No.27 Squadron re-formed at Scampton on 1 April. The squadron received its first B.2 serial XJ823 three weeks after reforming, followed by four more during the next six months. In October both squadrons flew to the United States to participate in America's national air defence exercise, Skyshield, acting as part of the 'attacking' forces. Four Vulcan B.2s of No.83 Squadron flew in from the north at 56,000ft – well above the USAF SAC bombers, and penetrated the defences while fighter interceptors were dealing with the SAC aircraft. Similarly, No.27 Squadron's aircraft penetrated successfully from the Caribbean area.

While probably not representative of an operational sortie in the European theatre, it did provide valuable training for the crews soon to receive the new Blue Steel weapon. By the beginning of 1962 No.617 Squadron had achieved emergency operational capability with Blue Steel and would have been equipped with the weapon had the Cuban Missile Crisis of that autumn developed into all-out war. In company with SAC, the RAF's V-Force was brought to a high state of readiness at this time, but the then Prime Minister, Harold Macmillan, would not give authorisation for the C-in-C of Bomber Command to disperse the force.

RAF Scampton actually became the first B.2 Wing when No.617 Squadron converted to the B.2 from August 1961, when it received its first B.2 serial XL318. By March 1962 No.617 Squadron had received a further six B.2 aircraft.

The third Vulcan Wing and second B.2 Wing was established at RAF Coningsby from March 1962. The first squadron to arrive was No.9, which reformed on 1 March having disbanded its E.E. Canberra B.6s there the previous summer. The squadron received its first Vulcan B.2 serial XL385 the following month and three more came during the next three months.

During this time, No.12 Squadron also reformed at Coningsby. Like No.9 Squadron, 12 Squadron had also operated Canberra B.6s until the previous summer when it disbanded to await the arrival of the Vulcan B.2. The third squadron to complete the Coningsby Wing was No.35 Squadron, which reformed in December bringing to a close a major re-organisation of Bomber Command's front-line Vulcan squadrons. The build-up of the new V-Force was complete.

Although much more would be done in the years ahead to enable the Vulcan to fulfil its task of maintaining Britain's nuclear deterrent, no period was busier for Bomber Command planners than the five years immediately after the Vulcan first entered operational service in 1957.

By the end of 1962 Bomber Command possessed ninety-four Vulcan bombers (45 B.1/B.1As and 49 B.2s) and the force had divided into three Vulcan Wings of three squadrons per wing. The Vulcan force on 31 December 1962 was:

Vulcan B.2 BS, serial XL318, completed in August 1961, served with No.617 Squadron No.230 OCU and No.27 Squadron. Function, mating and compatibility checks are in progress during loading of a Blue Steel Mk.1 stand-off missile beneath the bomber, while it was part of No.617 Squadron's inventory at RAF Scampton. On retirement XL318 was delivered to the RAF Museum, Hendon, north London, as 8733M in February 1982.

No.617 Squadron Vulcan B.2 and crew about to leave their Scampton base on a 'Lone Ranger' mission in the autumn of 1961. (*Lincolnshire Echo*)

Vulcan B.2 BS, serial XM595, completed in August 1963, served with Nos 617, 27 and 35 Squadrons. Produced as a Blue Steel Mk.1 carrier, it is seen here in low-level camouflage for 'pop-up' delivery of the weapon following its modification for this purpose. XM595 was scrapped in 1982. (*Lincolnshire Echo*)

Vulcan B.2 BS, serial XL389, completed in July 1962, served with 230 OCU, Nos 617, 9, 44 and 101 Squadrons, until it was sold as scrap in 1981. Here it can be seen at the RAF Abingdon, Oxfordshire, Battle of Britain Air Day on 13 September 1980 in 101 Squadron markings with the City of Lincoln shield on the tail fin. (Mike Hooks)

Vulcan B.2, serial XM647, was completed in April 1964 and served with Nos 9, 35, 44 and 50 Squadrons.It is seen here in 44 Squadron markings on static display in June 1980. XM647 was sold as scrap in 1985. (Mike Hooks)

One of the early series production Vulcan B.2s with new Phase 2 wing lifts off at RAE Farnborough in the early 1960s. (Ron Smith)

Coningsby Wing (Vulcan B.2s)

No.9 Squadron (at full strength in February 1963)
No.12 Squadron
No.35 Squadron (did not reform until 1 November 1962)

Scampton Wing (Vulcan B.2s)

No.27 Squadron
No.83 Squadron
No.617 Squadron

Waddington Wing (Vulcan B.1/B.1As)

No.44 Squadron
No.50 Squadron
No.101 Squadron

RAF Finningley (Vulcan B.1/B.1A and B.2s)

No.230 Operational Conversion Unit (OCU)
A Flight (B.1/B.1A)
B Flight (B.2)

Bomber Command Development Unit (BCDU) Trials Flight

Vulcan B.1 XA907, B.1A XA907, XL391 B.2 BS

Vulcan B.1 XA907 arrived in June 1961. Low-level trials were a priority, but the development of a low-level bomb-sight for the co-pilot and tests of a new jammer and later Blue Steel were also high priority. The Vulcans remained at the BCDU until October 1966 when, with no updated aircraft to spare, the unit reverted to 'borrowing' aircraft as required. The unit was absorbed by the Central Tactics and Trials Organisation on 31 December 1968.

In February 1961 the then Defence Minister declared, 'as it stands at the moment, Bomber Command is capable, by itself, of crippling the industrial power of any aggressor nation'. It was also announced that it was planned to deploy Skybolt, an air-launched strategic nuclear weapon built by Douglas with a range of over 1,000 miles, to safeguard the V-Force from the ever-increasing Soviet surface-to-air (SAM) threat. It was announced that Skybolt would be available to the squadrons by the mid-1960s after it had entered service with the USAF Strategic Air Command (SAC) at the end of 1963 and the RAF missiles were to be fitted with British warheads. For 'free-fall' operations the 10,000lb Blue Danube and Violet Club were being replaced by Yellow Sun Mk.1 and the lighter weight American nuclear weapons, two of which would fit into the bomb-bay of a V-bomber. The introduction of Blue Steel was also well advanced and the Scampton Wing was to commence work-up as the Vulcan Blue Steel unit.

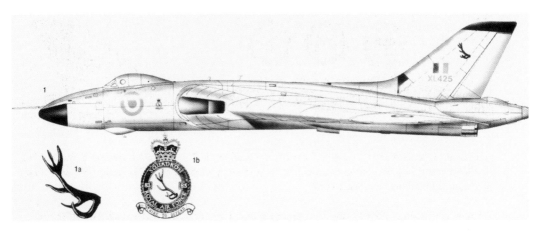

1) Vulcan B.2, serial XL425, was completed in August 1962 and allocated to No.83 Squadron at RAF Scampton in 1964. The aircraft were finished in anti-nuclear flash overall white with national markings also in anti-flash pale colours, with pale blue serial XL425. This plane also served with Nos 617 and 27 Squadrons and was modified to carry Blue Steel. It was eventually sold as scrap in 1982. (Modelaid AF1)

1a) Squadron motif – an antler on fin in brownish red.
Squadron motto – *Strike to Defend*.
1b) Squadron crest on front fuselage is a brown antler with yellow details.

2) Vulcan B.2, serial XL321, was completed in January 1962 and allocated to No.617 'Dambusters' Squadron, Scampton, in 1964. Aircraft finish as for (1) with pale red flashes on fin. Squadron Leader's pennant is displayed on forward fuselage to the rear of the squadron crest.

2a) Squadron crest containing red lightning flashes on a white sky, yellow-breached dam and blue/white water. No.617 Squadron's Vulcan B.1 carried only a small squadron badge on the fuselage sides beneath the pilot's cockpit. When the V-force changed to a low-level strike role the bombers were camouflaged, and for a while no squadron markings were carried. Later, a few aircraft had 'day-glow' red 'lightning flashes' cut from plastic sheet's affixed, but these proved to not be weather-resistant and were replaced in 1977 by a white diamond with a pale blue outline, encompassing red flashes, and yellow 'dam walls' – a representation of the squadron badge. XL321 also served with No.27 Squadron, 230 OCU, Nos 35, 44, and 50 Squadrons and was modified to carry Blue Steel.
Squadron motto – *Après moi, le déluge* (After me, the flood). (Modelaid AF1)

3) Vulcan B.1A serial XA910 completed as a B.1 in October 1957 with the Waddington Bomber Wing in 1966. Aircraft in gloss dark green/medium sea grey with white underside with standard red-white-blue national markings and black serial.

3a) Shows repetition of serial on inside of undercarriage doors, as well as station and pooled aircraft squadron badges (Nos 44, 50 and 101) on crew entry door.
3b) Enlarged squadron badges.
No.44's elephant is grey on green grass.
Squadron motto – *Fulmina regis justa* (The King's thunderbolts are righteous).
No.50's cloak is red, white and grey with yellow sword, cord and tassels.
Squadron motto – *From defence to attack*.
No.101's lion is yellow with red mouth, on a grey tower with black details.
Squadron motto – *Mens agitat molem* (Mind over matter).

XA910 also served with 230 OCU and as a ground instructional aircraft until it was scrapped. (Modelaid AF1)

4) Vulcan B.2, serial XM607 (which flew three Black Buck missions in 1982), was completed in December 1963, allocated to the Waddington Bomber Wing in November 1971. Aircraft finish as for XA910 with No.1 (Bomber) Group's panther head on front fuselage (enlarged at 4a) in black/grey/white, with red tongue, white teeth and yellow outline and eyes. The City of Lincoln shield (4b) on the fin is white with black outline, red cross and yellow fleur-de-lis (panther marking faces forward on both sides of the fuselage). XM607 served with Nos 35, 44, 9 and 101 Squadrons; after its Falklands service it was placed on static display at RAF Waddington (8779M) in January 1983. (Modelaid AF1)

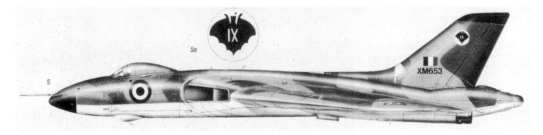

5) Vulcan B.2, serial XM653, completed in August 1964, served with No.9 Squadron, RAF Cottesmore, and is seen here in January 1968. Finish as (3 & 4) with dark green bat and white roman numeral 'IX', on a white disc displayed on the fin (5a). At Waddington the station badge (City of Lincoln Arms) eventually appeared on the fin along with a green bat on a yellow disc.

Squadron motif – a bat.

Squadron motto – *Per noctem volamus* (Through the night we fly).

XM653 also served with Nos 101 and 44 Squadrons until sold as scrap in 1981. (Modelaid AF1)

6) Vulcan B.2, serial XM606, completed in December 1963, is seen here with the Scampton Bomber Wing in April 1969. Camouflage finish with small black elephant on white disc on fin (6a). 6b shows repetition of serial on undercarriage doors as well as station badge and pooled aircraft squadron badges. (Nos 27, 83 and 617 – enlarged at 6c) on crew entry hatch. No.27 Squadron's elephant is black, No.83's antler is black, No.617's flashes are 'day-glo' red. Squadron numbers near motifs on the undercarriage entry hatch door are in light blue. XM606 also served with Nos 12, 101 and 9 Squadrons and was presented to Barksdale AFB, USA, in June 1982. (Modelaid AF1)

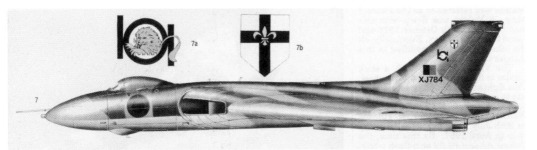

7) Vulcan B.2, serial XJ784, completed in March 1961, served with No.101 Squadron at RAF
Waddington and is seen here in 1982. Camouflage finish now matt dark green/medium sea grey with
light aircraft grey undersides. Toned down blue/red national markings and black serial Squadron motif
on fin.

7a) Is a red 'stylised' '101' on camouflage background, with pale yellow lion on white battlements. Lion
faces forward on both sides of fin. City of Lincoln shield.
7b) Also on the fin above and is slightly to the right of the '101' motif. XJ784 also served as trials aircraft,
then with 230 OCU, and Nos 9, 44 and 101 Squadrons until being sold as scrap in 1982.
Squadron motto – *Mens agitat molem* (Mind over matter). (Modelaid AF1)

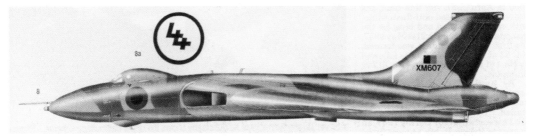

8) Vulcan B.2, serial XM607, of No.44 Squadron as it appeared in May/June 1982 in matt dark green/
medium sea grey with dark sea grey undersides. Toned down blue/red national markings and black
serial. This aircraft earned great fame for its participation in Operation Corporate 'Black Buck' missions
in the South Atlantic in 1982.

8a) No.44 Squadron motif as applied on the fin in black/white before and after the war. Lincoln shield
(matt) was also displayed as for 7b. (Modelaid AF1)

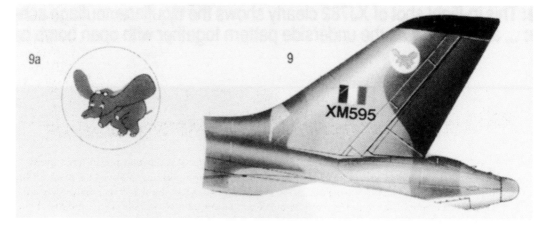

9) Detail of Vulcan B.2 XM595, completed August 1963. Seen here with No.27 Squadron at RAF Scampton, with a representation of Walt Disney's 'Dumbo' on the fin, as in September 1971. Aircraft in dark green/medium sea grey/white finish. Dumbo (9a) is green with white eyes and goggles, and pink feet, on a white disc. Operating in the low-level tactical role the aircraft carried a 'thimble' terrain-avoidance radome on the nose as for 4, 6, 7 and 8. National markings and roundels were in high-visibility red, white and blue. XM595 also served with Nos 617 and 35 Squadrons and was modified to carry Blue Steel. XM595 was sold as scrap in 1982. (Modelaid AF1)

10) Detail of Vulcan B.2 XM574 completed June 1963, with No.617 Squadron, with markings as they appeared in June 1970. Overall finish as for XM595 with 'day-glo' red lightning flash on fin. The aircraft now carried a terrain-following radar (TFR) thimble on the nose. (Modelaid AF1)

11) Vulcan B.1, serial XA897, completed in July 1956, the ninth series production aircraft was delivered in all-over silver finish with black radome and tail-fin top. National markings included the massive 54in high-visibility roundel and 18in-high black serial and City of Lincoln shield. Unfortunately it was this aircraft that crashed at London Heathrow Airport on its return from New Zealand on 1 October 1956. (Modelaid AF1)

12) Vulcan B.2 BB serial XM607, No.44 Squadron, RAF Waddington, in 1982 during the Falklands Black Buck operations. The operational colour scheme for the mission was as detailed here with dark green and sea grey over light aircraft grey under-surfaces and toned-down national markings in line with the requirements for the night flights to the South Atlantic. The three raids the aircraft flew are reflected in the three small black iron bombs on the nose. (Modelaid AF1)

Left: Formation of the Vulcan Wings, with pooled aircraft, lead the squadron badges to be displayed on the crew entry door. Those of Nos 44, 50 and 101 Squadrons are seen here on Vulcan B.1A, serial XA910, at Luqa, Malta, on 19 October 1966. (Modelaid AF1)

Below: Vulcan B.2, serial XL384, completed in March 1962, was one of the first B.2s to be used by 230 OCU. XL384 saw service with the Scampton and Waddington Wings, was a ground instructional aircraft and was also modified to carry Blue Steel. Following a heavy landing accident in August 1971 it was finally struck-off-charge in May 1985! (Mike Hooks)

TFR radome
A tiny pimple radome mounted below the inflight-refuelling probe serves the Texas Instruments Terrain Avoidance Radar.

XM600

Undercarriage
The main undercarriage units consist of eight wheeled bogies which retract inwards into the wing roots. The mainwheel undercarriage bays also housed the refuelling and defuelling panels.

Avro Vulcan B.Mk 2 of No. 617 Squadron, 'The Dambusters', based at RAF Scampton, soon after the withdrawal of 'Blue Steel'. This aircraft is seen in low-level camouflage, although it retains anti-flash white undersurfaces and high conspicuity roundels. A stylised version of the squadron's bursting dam badge is carried on the fin, and there is a No. 1 (Bomber) Group Panther's head on the nose, indicating participation in a 'Giant Voice' bombing competition.

Powerplants
The Vulcan B.Mk 2 was powered by four Bristol Siddeley Olympus turbojets, each rated at 20,000 lb st. These engines were buried in the deep wing roots, fed by simple rectangular intakes in the leading edge and exhausting through simple jet pipes on the trailing edge.

Wing pylons
Many Vulcan B.Mks 2s were built with attachments and wiring for underwing pylons to carry the Skybolt air-launched missile. The SR.Mk 2s of No. 27 Squadron sometimes used these pylons to carry air sampling pods, and the aircraft deployed to the Falklands used them for carrying Shrike anti-radar missile and ECM pods.

Cockpit
The Vulcan was regarded as a superb pilot's machine, despite its size. Superb handling was complemented by fighter-type control columns, in place of the yokes usually fitted to large aircraft. The captain and co-pilot at side-by-side on Martin Baker ejection seats, but the aft facing navigators and AEO were denied the luxury of 'bang seats', supposedly because it would have been too difficult to instal them.

Armament
The Vulcan's capacious bomb bay, like that of the Valiant, could accommodate up to 21 conventional 1,000-lb bombs, or a variety of different nuclear weapons. Yellow Sun was a free-fall nuclear weapon designed for delivery in a pop-up manoeuvre, while WE.177 was a retarded weapon which could be delivered in a laydown attack.

Wing
The Vulcan's huge wing was increased in area by 410 sq ft with the B.Mk 2, with a 12-ft increase in the overall span, and an extended leading edge with a characteristic double kink. The new wing generated more lift, and gave a much improved high altitude performance. The range of the B.Mk 2 was increased from 3,000 to 4,600 miles.

(*Take Off*, Part Works)

The decision to buy Skybolt led to Avro trying to develop and sell an improved Stage 6 Vulcan bomber with Olympus 23 engines, including a simple reheat system giving 23,500lb thrust, a new wing (over 117ft span) with a gross all-up weight of over 350,000lb capable of carrying up to six Skybolts. Had this aircraft been developed, it would have been designated Vulcan B.3 and would also have been capable of carrying a conventional bomb load.

In January 1961 XH563 flew to California in the United States for Skybolt compatibility trials, and then on to Wright-Paterson AFB, in Dayton, Ohio, for further trials. In November, XH537 made the first flight with a dummy Skybolt missile under each wing, followed in December by a dummy practice drop from 45,000ft.

Further trials were carried out by XH538 at Elgin AFB in Florida. However, the Skybolt programme suffered major setbacks resulting in failures during live firings and at the end of 1962 the project was cancelled by the United States government.

Throughout the 1950s experiments with air-launched guided bombs had proved in the main unsuccessful, and a number of projects such as Blue Boar had been cancelled, some as early as 1954. It was decided that what was required was an air-launched bomb capable of being released up to 100 miles from the target in any weather by day or night. This led to the development of the Blue Steel, a weapon capable of carrying a megaton warhead and the H2S Mk.9A radar, this machine was allied to a Navigation and Bombing Computer Mk.2 to form the NBS Mk.1 used to guide the bombers to their target. NBS computed track and ground-speed from the H2S radar returns, and could be used to fly the bomber and release the bomb at the correct moment. The route which the aircraft would follow to its target had been planned in advance to avoid the known Soviet air defence radars and the embryonic, but continually expanding, SAM forces,that were constantly monitored from friendly or international airspace around the Iron Curtain by 'ferret' flights. A number of these flights emanated from the UK with both the RAF (using American RB-45Cs, operating from RAF Sculthorpe) and subsequently USAF Lockheed U-2s operating from RAF Alconbury.

A contract had been awarded to Avro's Weapons Research Division in 1956 to develop Blue Steel, with the weapon to be carried by both the Vulcan and the Victor. It was developed by Avro at Woodford and trials began in 1957. In 1959 Vulcan serial XA903 became the trials aircraft for further development. Although some trials were carried out in the UK, further tests were carried out at the Maralinga firing range in the north of South Australia, using serials XH538 and XH539.

Early problems encountered with Blue Steel came about as a result of the limited range of the weapon. It was, therefore, decided to develop a replacement, the Blue Steel Mk.2, with four Bristol Siddeley ramjets and two solid-fuel booster rockets.

It was estimated that the missile would be capable of Mach 3 at 70,000ft and an increased range of between 800 and 1,000 miles. However, about the same time as development on the 'Mk.2' weapon began, the British Government cancelled the Mk.2 Project in December 1959 in favour of the American Douglas Skybolt.

This now meant that two projects, Blue Streak and Blue Steel Mk.2, had been cancelled in favour of the American weapon, and consequently, when Skybolt was also cancelled, Britain was left with a large gap in its nuclear deterrent capability.

Bomber Command's V-Force was left with only the Blue Steel Mk.1 as its only stand-off weapon.

Initially it was planned for 1960 to be the in-service date for Blue Steel. However, it soon became apparent that production delays and increasing costs meant that Blue Steel would not enter service on time. In fact, it transpired that Blue Steel would not enter service until 1963–64, therefore becoming less economic, and so the decision was made to reduce the order from seventy-five to fifty-seven weapons.

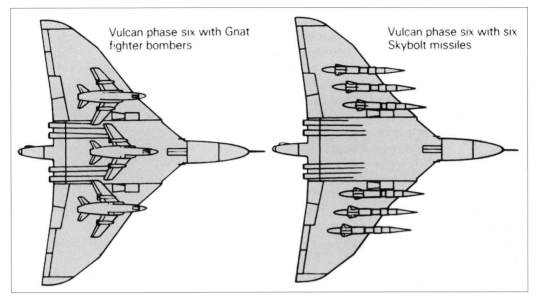

Vulcan phase six with Gnat fighter bombers

Vulcan phase six with six Skybolt missiles

Even before Blue Steel entered service it was becoming increasingly obvious that penetrating even peripheral Soviet defences would be difficult and that a stand-off weapon with an even greater range was clearly necessary. Before Skybolt was ordered in 1960 to equip the Vulcan force, the RAF considered fitting nuclear-armed Folland Gnat fighters below an upgraded big-wing Vulcan. To carry the Douglas Skybolt, a big-wing Vulcan capable of carrying six missiles was proposed with the intended designation B.3. Eventually, instead, it was decided to fit two Skybolts under the wings of modified Avro Vulcan B.2 variants. (*Take Off*, Part Works)

Trials of Avro Blue Steel began with XA903 at Woodford in 1959. Further trials were flown over Maralinga, in the north of South Australia; the trials aircraft serials XH538 and XH539 were based at RAAF Edinburgh, about eighteen miles north of Adelaide, the capital of that region. (Mike Hooks)

Early trials of the weapon in Australia were not a great success, although the decision was made in 1961 to modify three Vulcan B.2 squadrons at RAF Scampton to carry the new weapon.

To carry the missile semi-recessed under the fuselage meant that the Vulcan's internal fuselage and bomb-bay doors had to be modified (giving rise to the B.2A Vulcan). From July 1961 these modifications were included during the building stage at Avro's Woodford plant and from March 1962 all the Vulcans off the production line were powered by Olympus Mk.301 engines.

Trials during 1962 were more successful, and as a result No.617 Squadron began training ready to receive Blue Steel, although it was February 1963 before the squadron was declared operational in its new role. They were to be followed by Nos 27 and 83 Squadrons later in the year.

The production Blue Steel delivered to the RAF was powered by an Armstrong Siddeley Stentor (16,000lb thrust) rocket engine. Its launch profile was to drop 300ft from the launch aircraft before the initial boost and main motor ignited. The missile would then climb to an altitude of about 70,000ft and accelerate to Mach 2.5.

The inertial navigation system meant that the missile no longer relied on the launch aircraft for information and guidance to the target. Over a distance of 100 nautical miles it could be relied upon to strike within 100 yards of the target – quite accurate enough for a nuclear weapon!

The end of the Indonesian confrontation did not bring about the complete withdrawal of Vulcan bombers from the Far East, and two aircraft detachments, by way of a 'show of force', were maintained at the RAAF base at Butterworth, Malaya. (*Take Off*, Part Works)

Vulcan B.2, serial XM605, completed in December 1963, served with Nos 9, 101 and 50 Squadrons. XM605 is seen here at Goose Bay, Labrador, for training in low-level flying. On retirement in September 1981 XM605 was presented to Castle AFB, Texas, USA. (Mike Hooks)

By the end of 1963 the two other Vulcan B.2 squadrons of the Scampton Wing, Nos 27 and 83, had completed conversion. Training followed in 1964 by two Victor squadrons, Nos 100 and 139, based at RAF Wittering. By then, the RAF had twenty-four Vulcans and twelve Victors equipped to carry Blue Steel.

In order to get closer to the target, a bomber carrying Blue Steel would have to fly at low-level to avoid detection, not only by any tracking radar, but also, and probably more importantly, any SAM system.

When Indonesia entered into military confrontation with what was then the UK Protectorate of Malaysia, H.P. Victors were despatched in December 1963 to Butterworth, Malaya, and Tengah, Singapore, as a reminder that Britain still had a powerful air force. Some months later, four Vulcan bombers were sent to RAF Gan, a British outpost on a tiny island in the Indian Ocean, to reinforce the threat, and Indonesia backed down. The Far East detachments continued, however, with Vulcans replacing the Victors; a pair of Vulcans maintained at 'readiness' at Butterworth provided valuable crew training and helped prevent any further unrest in the area.

Vulcan bombers carried a crew of five; however, seven crew members are seen here at Scampton boarding an aircraft detaching to Goose Bay on a low-level flying training detachment. (*Take Off*, Part Works)

At about this time American bombs and Yellow Sun Mk.1s were withdrawn from the V-Force and replaced by Red Beard as the British tactical weapon. H.P. Victor and Vulcan crews commenced training in low-level operations in support of NATO, although the aircraft remained available to Britain for use in 'out of NATO' areas. The arrangement was implemented by way of Sunspot detachments of four or six aircraft on Central Treaty Organisation (CENTO) exercises flown from Iranian bases, and 'Lone Ranger' flights. The latter involved a single V-bomber and provided a little light relief for crews from the tedium of squadron life in the UK, a life that consisted mainly of seemingly endless QRAs and alert exercises, especially after the cancelling of the Skybolt missile and the downgrading of the force.

On the other hand, the force was steadily growing in operational strength and at the end of 1963 three Valiant, six Victor and nine Vulcan bomber squadrons were available. In February 1964 it was disclosed the V-Force was at its operational peak, with 159 aircraft (fifty Valiants, thirty-nine Victors and seventy Vulcans) in sixteen squadrons; nevertheless, it was still intended to increase the size of the in-flight refuelling force, a move which would lead to a corresponding reduction in the size of the bomber force and thus free-up a number of Valiants to be converted for tanking. Of the available bombers, 60 per cent had to be available within six hours of an alert and 80 per cent within twelve hours – a very demanding requirement, but practice alerts proved it possible!

The whole V-Force, with the majority of the fleet comprising Avro Vulcans, was now trained for both high and low-level operations, equipped with Blue Steel for high-level use and a variety of bombs designed for low-level release.

To practice over terrain similar to that covering large parts of the Soviet Union, much of the low-level training was carried out in Canada under the control of the Bomber Command Detachment at Goose Bay, Labrador. Crews would generally fly three or four approved routes during each visit.

Immediately after Golf Club, a Malayan air defence exercise held in February 1964, No.10 Squadron with H.P. Victor B.1s returned to the UK and was disbanded, leaving only Nos 15, 55 and 57 Squadrons (all with Victor B.1s) in theatre to deal with the Indonesian 'confrontation', a conflict that began to worsen in September just at the time the Victors were being withdrawn and replaced by Vulcan B.2s of the Coningsby Wing (Nos 9, 12 and 35 Squadrons), renamed the Cottesmore Wing when relocated to Cottesmere in November 1964.

5

Cold War Strategy

Following the Vulcan Wing reorganisations, the Air Staff decreed that in the event of an emergency, squadron engineers should be capable of having 60 per cent serviceability within six hours and 80 per cent within twelve hours, so aircraft were never dismantled to such an extent that the required percentage could not be re-assembled within that time schedule. With training flights to Canada, Goose Bay and the USA, where Bomber Command took part in SAC's annual bombing competition and various flag-waving sorties to other parts of the world at frequent intervals, the group's planes were widely dispersed around the globe. Neverthless, they were bound together by a strong sense of shared heritage, something that was only strengthened when all the squadrons received orders that, at times of crisis, they should return to the UK as quickly as possible. With this plan in place, even allowing for a worst case scenario, Bomber Command claimed they would always have at least 110 strategic bombers available to go to war within twelve hours.

It had been identified early in the Vulcan's career that, if necessary, the V-Force would be given very little time to respond in the event of a nuclear attack against the UK; it was estimated that as little as three minutes would be available to get the bombers off the ground and safely away so clearly efficiency and time-responsiveness were issues that had to be continually addressed.

As a result, in 1962 the format changed to QRA: (Quick Reaction Alert), and, as a result, Operational Readiness Platforms (ORPs) were built at airfields in order to minimise take-off time. From then on, each squadron was tasked with having one bomber at fifteen minutes' readiness throughout the year, although considerably more would be standing 'ready' if the international situation demanded. America could afford the luxury of 'standing airborne patrols', but at least the RAF could support its bombers with its own in-flight refuelling tankers, in a similar manner to the Boeing KC 135As attached to each SAC Bombardment Wing.

Simultaneous engine starting meant that reaction time was eventually reduced to two minutes. However, this was very much dependent on aircraft being manned by the crew at a 'cockpit ready' state. To minimise the problem of having too many aircraft at just one or two bases, ten airfields were developed to enable the V-Force to be dispersed when necessary. If the international situation ever deteriorated to such a state that war appeared inevitable, Bomber Command HQ at High Wycombe would be told to disperse the whole V-Force in groups of four. The question of when such an order might be given of course depended on the politicians.

Development work at the dispersal airfields included construction of runways 9,000ft long, 200ft wide and which would also have to be capable of withstanding the weight of fully laden bombers weighing up to 200,000lb. Additionally, hard standings were provided for up to sixteen aircraft along with support equipment and refuelling facilities.

Vulcans on the Operational Readiness Platform (ORP), at RAF Finningley, Yorkshire, in 1962. The aircraft were ready to roll straight on to the runway. Everything attached to the bomber on the ORP, such as the ground power unit and tele-scramble link, was designed to release automatically as the aircraft rolled forward on to the runway. On practice scrambles, in their efforts to get airborne as quickly as possible V-bombers were known to crush the matchwood chocks left in their way. (*Take Off*, Part Works)

In the 1960s the V-force maintained a constant twenty-four-hour state of readiness, with nuclear-armed aircraft ready to go at a moment's notice. Here a No.83 Squadron aircraft is being prepared for a night sortie. (*Take Off*, Part Works)

V-bomber force nuclear alert exercises often meant many hours spent at remote dispersal airfields throughout the UK. These nuclear-armed, white-painted bombers relied on their speed, high-altitude performance, and comprehensive ECM suite to get through to their targets unscathed, although as the Soviets introduced ever more capable SAMs the writing was on the wall for V-bomber high-altitude operations. This 'dispersed' Vulcan is a No.230 OCU aircraft. (*Take Off*, Part Works)

Above: To transport V-force crews to and from the dispersal airfields the RAF bought a small fleet of Beagle Bassett light twin-engined communications aircraft. Subsequently, these aircraft proved totally inadequate for the job and were used as squadron 'hacks' until they were withdrawn from use and sold on the civil light-plane market. (*Take Off*, Part Works)

Left: The cornerstone of the effectiveness of the V-force lay in the rapid reaction time to deploy the bombers on their mission, and this relied largely on the capability provided by the Ballistic Missile Early Warning radar station at Fylingdales on the north Yorkshire moors. Here, two Vulcan B.2s – one the ubiquitous XH558 – of Cottesmore Wing fly past the station's distinctive 'golf ball' antennas. The three Cottesmore-based squadrons were armed at this time with the WE177 lay-down nuclear bomb, while Waddington's Vulcans had the ageing Yellow Sun and Scampton had Blue Steel.

Main V-bomber bases and dispersal airfield locations in 1962. (*Take Off*, Part Works)

In addition to the ten selected major bases, a number of other RAF airfields throughout the UK were made available for V-Force dispersal if required. This meant that the dispersal plan for the force would have made the bombers as immune to attack as possible under the circumstances.

Main V-bomber bases

RAF Coningsby, Lincolnshire:	Avro Vulcans
RAF Cottesmore, Rutland:	Avro Vulcans and H.P. Victors
RAF Finningley, Yorkshire:	Avro Vulcans, H.P. Victors and Vickers Valiants
RAF Gaydon, Warwickshire:	Vickers Valiants
RAF Honington, Suffolk:	H.P. Victors
RAF Marham, Norfolk:	Vickers Valiants and H.P. Victors
RAF Scampton, Lincolnshire:	Avro Vulcans
RAF Wittering, Northamptonshire:	Vickers Valiants and H.P. Victors
RAF Wyton, Huntingdonshire:	Vickers Valiants and H.P. Victors

Additional V-bomber dispersal airfields

RAF Aldergrove N.I., RAE Bedford, A&AEE Boscombe Down, RAF Brawdy, Burtonwood, RAF Cranwell, RAF Elvington, Filton, RAF Kemble, RAF Kinloss, RAF Leconfield, RAF Leeming, RAF Leuchars, RAE Llanbedr, RAF Macrihanish, RAF Manston, RAF Middleton St George, RAE Pershore, Prestwick, RAF St Mawgan, RAF Shawbury, RAF Tarrant Rushton, RAF Valley, RNAS Yeovilton.

To transport crews to and from dispersal airfields, the RAF bought a fleet of twenty Beagle Basset five and eight-seat light twin-engined communications aircraft. These could carry a complete V-bomber crew, but had insufficient range to reach some of the further dispersal airfields; in any case, V-bombers tended to be deployed to the dispersal airfields with their crews on an 'as required' basis, and there was seldom any need to change crews over, so the Bassets were not often used in their intended role. Eventually the Bassets were withdrawn from use and sold on the civil market.

To complement the dispersal plan, an extra two warning plans had been devised to ensure maximum operational readiness was maintained at all times.

The Strategic Warning Plan gave the force twenty-four hours' notice to bring 75 per cent of its aircraft to 'combat readiness' and this was broken down further to 20 per cent within two hours, 40 per cent within four hours and 60 per cent within eight hours.

The Tactical Warning Plan meant that the bombers had to be at fifteen minutes' readiness for up to one week or forty minutes' readiness for up to one month. These warnings were both expensive and tiring for the air and ground-crews, and the system was improved in 1962 when QRA was introduced. The QRA system was further enhanced when the Fylingdales Early Warning Station became operational in 1963.

Had events forced the Government's hand and the bombers dispersed, each quartet of aircraft would have stayed at fifteen minutes' readiness. They would have been 'combat checked', meaning all pre-flight checks would been completed up to engine start; from then on crews and their support staff would have to pass their time in the immediate vicinity of their special caravans by chatting, reading, playing cards, board games or anything to relieve the inevitable nervous tension. If the situation continued to deteriorate the 'readiness state' would have moved up the scale and 'cockpit readiness' would have been ordered, when the aircrews would have had to leave the confines of their caravan, sprint to their aircraft and strap themselves in.

Each bomber was connected to reality by an umbilical tele-scramble link to the bomber controller at RAF High Wycombe, and on command from the war room in London he would have instructed his C-in-C to order the V-Force to start engines and then to 'scramble'. On airfields all along the east coast of the UK from Cornwall to Scotland, V-bomber engines would have started simultaneously and the aircraft taken-off in quick succession until, long before four minutes had passed, there would be nothing left to show where just a few minutes earlier they had stood in silence, save for some turbulent and darkened air and the pungent smell of burnt jet exhaust and aviation fuel.

As the bombers climbed higher and higher into the sky the small pilots' windows would have been covered by the anti-flash blinds. Roller blinds for the windscreens and metal shields for the canopy windows were fitted to all the V-bombers to protect the crew from nuclear explosion flash and thermal radiation; they were put in place after take-off as there was no longer any need for the crew to see outside of their respective compartments.

From all along the east coast of Britain the V-Force would have roared away to specific rendezvous points as laid down by Bomber Command. Radio silence would be maintained to prevent detection. The crews had no need to communicate with each other as they had trained to go about their work in complete silence. The blinds would be down behind the pilots, leaving the rear crew feeling as though they were 'facing backwards in a broom cupboard at midnight', but this would not stop navigational data being fed directly to the autopilot while the co-pilot monitored the fuel state on a slide rule with renewed intensity. Fuses could blow, equipment malfunction, even engines fail – it would all need to be dealt with and sorted out immediately, as the situation dictated. Most systems were duplicated so as to permit the bomber to fly on regardless, while the Navigation Plotter could work by 'astronomy' from the unjammable and infallible galaxy of stars if needs be. All the years of training to cope with equipment failures came to the fore, and there was really nowhere to go so long as the aircraft remained in the air and at least two engines kept running.

The great advantage of a manned bomber over an ICBM (Inter-Continental Ballistic Missile) is that the bomber can be recalled...

The Vulcan had basically been designed as a medium to high-altitude bomber. To train a pilot to fly at low-level is normally straightforward. But the Vulcan is a large aircraft and pilots would be expected to fly to targets in all weathers, by day and by night.

This was not to be the only problem associated with the change in ideas and tactics in the mid-1960s. Firstly, the airframe required strengthening to withstand the extra fatigue of low-level flying; secondly, new equipment was required to help crews penetrate heavy enemy defences at low level, e.g. terrain-following radar and passive electronic counter-measures; and, thirdly, it was necessary to modify Blue Steel so that it could be launched from below 1,000ft. This major modification to Blue Steel was far from easy but by mid-1964 it was available to the crews.

Following successful trials, the Blue Steel squadrons immediately began low-level training. The only aid to terrain-following at night and in bad weather was a minute radome on the tip of the bombers' nose. Introduced in 1966, this housed a General Dynamics obstruction-warning radar which alerted pilots aurally to high ground ahead. A more sophisticated radar-navigation aid was proposed, but it fell victim to the same philosophy that had prevented the three rear crew members from being retrospectively given ejection seats – the cost was estimated at about £100,000 per aircraft. The launch profile was modified so that the launch aircraft flew at low-level towards the target and at 25 miles from the target it 'popped up' to release the weapon.

The Blue Steel weapon then climbed to about 17,000ft and guided itself to the target. By the time the missile was entering the terminal and final phase of flight the launch aircraft was making good its escape from hostile territory at high speed and low altitude.

At this time the characteristic anti-flash paint scheme of the high-altitude bomber gave way to the dark green and grey camouflaged paint scheme of the low-level bomber, although it was to be another ten years before the brightly coloured 54in RAF roundels were 'toned down'.

This change in tactics was relevant not just for the delivery of Blue Steel but also for the rest of the Vulcan force.

The remaining B.1s were armed with 'free-fall' megaton-yield weapons (a lighter version of the Yellow Sun Mk.2 with Red Snow warheads) and the B.2s with either a new lay-down bomb, WE177 (developed from a low-yield retard bomb that originally equipped the Blackburn Buccaneer maritime strike bomber), or the Yellow Sun Mk.2.

In particular, the release of Yellow Sun meant exposing the aircraft to a high level of ground threat as the release technique involved 'popping-up' from low level to a height of about 12,000ft, releasing the weapon, and returning again to low level to escape enemy airspace without detection.

Training in low-level operations began in 1963 and took three years to complete. During the same period the RAF moved its second Vulcan B.2 Wing, which had been established at RAF Coningsby in 1962 with three squadrons – 9, 12 and 35 – to Cottesmore in November 1964. The last series production Vulcan B.2, serial XM657, was delivered to No.35 Squadron in January 1965.

By this time, most of the Vulcan B.1s had gone, although some remained in use for various trials programmes. Excluding the prototypes, XM657 was the eighty-ninth Vulcan B.2 to be built. Completed on 14 January 1965, it was delivered to No.35 Squadron the following day!

Meanwhile, following the enforced retirement of the Valiant, a combination of circumstances led to the Vulcan's role being extended still further. The Government's announcement of the cancellation of the BAC TSR-2 multi-role aircraft, at the height of Bomber Command's re-organisation, and with all the Vulcan B.2s delivered, led to the C-in-C of Bomber Command requesting from the C-in-C of the Far East Air Force (FEAF), a Vulcan reinforcement detachment for the area. This served to prove the flexibility and capabilities of those aircraft that remained at his disposal.

Following some high-powered diplomatic involvement, a 'no notice' Exercise Spherical was ordered on 26 April 1965, tasking No.35 Squadron with the deployment of eight Vulcan B.2s to Gan in the Indian Ocean. Thirty-two hours later all had arrived safely and were soon 'readied' to move on to Butterworth and Tengah. The exercise served to prove that they could have been fully operational in the Far East within sixty hours of receiving the order 'to go' at their Cottesmore base. More routine deployments, known as the Matterhorn Rotations, consisted of four aircraft on three-month detachments, which continued until the end of the Malaysian 'confrontation' (Operation Firedog) with Indonesia in August 1966. Although a heavy drain on Bomber Command resources at the time, it was good training for the crews in a more 'conventional' role.

By 1966 the Vulcan bomber contribution to the V-Force numbered nine operational squadrons:

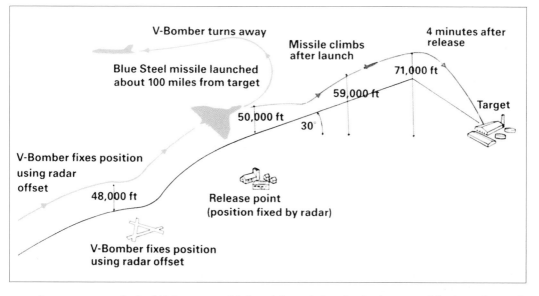

V-Bomber turns away

Missile climbs
after launch

4 minutes after
release

Blue Steel missile launched
about 100 miles from target

71,000 ft

59,000 ft

Target

50,000 ft

30

V-Bomber fixes position
using radar
offset

48,000 ft

Release point
(position fixed by radar)

V-Bomber fixes position
using radar offset

Improvements to Soviet SAM systems and fighter defences led to the development of the Avro Blue Steel with its own onboard inertial navigator. This permitted launch of the weapon about 100 miles from the target, allowing the carrier – a Vulcan or Victor – to 'stand-off' a considerable distance from the target.

Two Vulcan B.2s of the Finningley-based Bomber Development Unit (BDU) display the contrasting original high-level nuclear anti-flash white finish and the new low-level penetration camouflage.

Two Scampton Wing Vulcan B.2 Bs on a low-level tactical training sortie, with their high intensity landing lights on. One aircraft is equipped with an upgraded Stentor rocket-powered Blue Steel. (Mike Hooks)

The low-level role was also adopted by the standard Vulcan B.2 aircraft of the Waddington and Cottesmore Wings during 1964. (*Take Off*, Part Works)

Above: Vulcan B.2, serial XM653, completed in August 1964, was among the last batch built and was delivered to the Waddington Wing that year. (Mike Hooks)

Right: An impressive line-up of the Vulcan B.2s of No.44 Squadron in Singapore. Many foreign trips were 'Lone Rangers' conducted by a single aircraft but complete squadrons did sometimes deploy en masse. (Mike Hooks)

Vulcan B.2 BS, serial XL443, completed in October 1962, represents the ultimate in Avro Vulcan bomber development. The Blue Steel capable bomber was fully equipped with ECM pod, low-level terrain warning radar thimble and in-flight refuelling probe. (Mike Hooks)

Cottesmore Wing: Vulcan B.2 and WE177 lay-down bomb

No.9 Squadron: Vulcan B.2
No.12 Squadron: Vulcan B.2
No.35 Squadron: Vulcan B.2

Scampton Wing: Vulcan B.2 and Blue Steel

No.27 Squadron: Vulcan B.2 BS
No.83 Squadron: Vulcan B.2 BS
No.617 Squadron: Vulcan B.2 BS

Waddington Wing: Vulcan B.1A and Yellow Sun Mk.2

No.44 Squadron: Vulcan B.1A
No.50 Squadron: Vulcan B.1A
No.101 Squadron: Vulcan B.1A

Despite the end of the 'confrontation' with Indonesia in August 1966, Vulcans still continued to deploy periodically to the Far East on month-long four-aircraft Sunflower detachments, during which they often went to Darwin, in Australia's Northern Territory, for exercises with RAAF Mirage fighters. On one such detachment a Vulcan led a seven aircraft Mirage V-formation over Sydney Harbour.

On 29 April 1968 Bomber Command's disbandment parade was held at Scampton in the presence of Marshals of the RAF Viscount Portal, Sir Arthur 'Bomber' Harris and many other distinguished guests. The occasion marked Bomber Command's thirty-three years of operations as the country's premier offensive force and the merging of Bomber and Fighter Commands to form Strike Command with its headquarters to remain at RAF High Wycombe, Buckinghamshire.

Avro/HSA Blue Steel 100A nuclear-armed supersonic air-to-surface missile or stand-off bomb

Manufacturer:	The Weapons Research Division of A.V. Roe and Co. Ltd
Number ordered:	57
Powerplant:	One Bristol Siddeley Stentor rocket engine
Dimensions:	wing-span 13ft, fore-plane span 6ft 6in, length 35ft, maximum body diameter 4ft 2in
Weight:	16,500–17,000lb
Range:	100 miles
Maximum speed:	Mach 1.6 (estimated)
Test firings:	At the Aberporth, Wales and Woomera, South Australia ranges Two Vulcan B.2 trials aircraft (XH538 and XH539), based at RAAF Edinburgh, north of Adelaide, South Australia, during 1959 and 1960
Operational service:	1963–30 June 1969
Delivery system:	Avro Vulcan B.2 BS and Handley Page Victor B.2R

Although Blue Steel was developed into an excellent stand-off weapon, its limited range was eventually to count against it, but in the beginning its main drawback came on the ground. The Stentor rocket engine, for instance, was fuelled by High Test Peroxide (HTP) and kerosene, and the former needed to be handled with great care, as it was lethal stuff!

Unless strictly controlled and handled at all times in airtight containers with surgical standards of cleanliness it 'decomposed' of its own accord. Decomposition took the form of a violent eruption as the peroxide gave off oxygen at a fantastic rate, and it was for this reason that it was used to power the Stentor. At high altitudes the HTP was needed to make the kerosene burn, but on the ground, when loading the weapon on to the aircraft, a large water tank was always positioned nearby into which any personnel were instructed to dive if HTP leaked on them, otherwise they would burst into flames as the HTP mixed with the oxygen in the air.

Blue Steel was also a temperamental beast. Large sums of money had to be spent on air-conditioned workshops with heated floors so that the missiles could be 'cosseted' while they were serviced and stored, yet on many occasions it proved impossible to mate the weapon with its carrier. Loading and unloading Blue Steel was a complex task, requiring several different items of specialised equipment. In effect the ground tradesman had to match two complex and sophisticated aircraft together whilst ensuring they were compatible, and this was not always easy. The hydraulics, for instance, which were used to power the control surfaces and to drive the alternator which provided the missile's electrics, were located half in the aircraft and half in the weapon. Sometimes one refused to 'talk' to the other. There was also the problem of making sure that all the 471 electrical connections between the bomber and Blue Steel mated correctly. The missile was electrically connected to its carrier by three lanyard-operated disconnect connectors, each with 157 contacts. To ensure all these released simultaneously when the weapon fell away from the aircraft, the connections were not plugs and sockets but just 'buttons' that touched. Thus, if something vital did not 'touch' properly the missile would not work. Unfortunately it took two and a half hours to arm the missile and load it before compatibility checks could be carried out and if anything was then found to be wrong with either the aircraft or the missile, or, as sometimes happened, a serviceable missile refused to mate with a serviceable aircraft, there was no question of just carrying out repairs because the missile had to be removed and go back to its air-conditioned workshop to go through the whole process of laborious checks and warhead unloading first.

Nevertheless, in the fullness of time most of the more irritating problems were sorted out and aircrews and ground-crews alike learned to live with the missile's quirks and unexplainable compatibility problems. One consolation was that once they were overcome, the weapon was almost certain to achieve a successful firing, with Air Marshal Sir Kenneth Cross in 1963 claiming, 'the Blue Steel can stand comparison with any other missile system being developed anywhere in the world'.

6

Phase-out and Run-down

In 1963 it was announced that the V-Force was to retire in 1968 when Polaris entered service. A year later this date was revised to 1972 and by 1968 the retirement date had been further postponed to 1975, with at least sixty Vulcan B.2s planned to remain in service until this time. During this period the RAF suffered another Vulcan bomber loss when XJ781, flying from Akrotiri, Cyprus, crash-landed at Shiraz, Iran, on 23 May 1973; the port undercarriage bogie had refused to lower, and although the crew survived what was a very good landing in the circumstances, XJ781 broke its back as its sliding progress down the runway was halted by it entering a deep storm drain. Being beyond economical repair, the bomber was abandoned and given to the Iranians, who reportedly broke it up to make beer cans!

From 1966 onwards, the three Waddington-based squadrons, Nos 44, 50 and 101, converted to Vulcan B.2s and the last of its B.1As departed to the scrap heap in January 1968.

The decision to opt for Polaris missiles (launched from Royal Navy submarines) as Britain's nuclear deterrent signalled the start of the process of reducing the size of Bomber Command at the end of 1967. The phasing out of Blue Steel between 1968 and 1970 led to No.12 Squadron at Cottesmore being disbanded on 31 December 1967. No.83 Squadron at Scampton disbanded on 31 August 1969 with Nos 27 and 617 Squadrons at Scampton reverting to the 'free-fall' conventional bombing role, while No.27 Squadron later assumed the additional role of maritime reconnaissance. Bomber Command QRA also ended in the summer of 1969 when the Royal Navy assumed responsibility for Britain's first line of strategic defence.

However, the invasion of Czechoslovakia in August 1968 by forces from the Warsaw Pact served as a reminder of the potential threat posed from Eastern Europe. The Government, realising that the main threat was still from behind the Iron Curtain and the Central/Eastern European region, announced early in 1968 that it was to withdraw British forces from bases east of Suez by 1971 in order to concentrate on the defence of Central and Western Europe. The strategic bombers were to be made available to SACEUR (Supreme Allied Commander Europe) NATO for operations in a tactical role.

On 21 December 1970, No.617 'Dambusters' Squadron flew the last Blue Steel sortie. This left the 'Dambusters' and No.27 Squadron at Scampton, and Nos 44, 50 and 101 Squadrons at Waddington to continue in the tactical service of NATO.

The return to tactical bombing saw the Giant Voice Flight formed at Waddington in 1973, where it remained until 1981 to train for the annual Strategic Air Command Bombing competitions held in America. The Giant Voice Flight had its own dedicated aircraft; these were the Vulcan B.2s XL391, XM599, XM606 and XM650 with their own distinctive No.1 (Bomber) Group panther's head nose marking either side of the forward fuselage to the rear of the distinctive 54in high-visibility red, white and blue roundel.

Above, opposite above and below: By 1968 most of the Vulcan B.1As that had been delivered more than ten years earlier were at RAF St Athan, Wales, for scrapping; among them were XA907, XH501, XH482 and XA912. XA912 (minus its complete nose assembly) was unique in that it served its entire ten-year front-line operational career with a single squadron, No.101. (Mike Hooks)

21 December 1970 heralded the end of an era for the RAF's V-bomber force when No.617 'Dambusters' Squadron flew the last Blue Steel operational sortie. (*Take Off*, Part Works)

Vulcan B.2, serial XM650, of the Giant Voice Flight at RAF Waddington in 1973. The unit trained for and participated in the Strategic Air Command bombing competitions in the United States. XM650 also served with Nos 12, 44 and 50 Squadrons until it was sold as scrap in 1984.

Avro Vulcan B.2 and English Electric Lightning supersonic air defence fighters were tasked with the defence of Cyprus. Equipped with WE177, Vulcans provided CENTO with a nuclear capability in the area. (Mike Hooks)

At home, Britain's offensive and defensive air assets at this time comprised the re-roled low-level Vulcan bomber, supersonic E.E. Lightning air defence fighter and McDonnell-Douglas Phantom interceptor, English Electric Canberra light-bomber, and the Blackburn Buccaneer low-level maritime strike bomber. (Mike Hooks)

Returning to the UK and the nations commitment to (SACUER) NATO finally brought a revised Vulcan bomber low-level 'European' camouflage scheme with the high-visibility national markings toned down. (Mike Hooks)

In addition to the long oblong fin top rear warning receiver (RWR) housing, Vulcan B.2 (MRR) reconnaissance variants carried a 'sniffer' for air sampling; the assembly was made from former Royal Navy Fleet Air Arm D.H. Sea Vixen fuel-drop tanks.

Above and below: By the early 1980s Vulcan B.2s were being scrapped. Completed in July 1960, XH559 still proudly displays its 230 OCU emblem. Having spent all its service career with the unit, it was sold for scrap in January 1982.

These were now the only Vulcan bombers left in the UK because, at the beginning of 1969, the sixteen B.2s of the Cottesmore Wing of Nos 9 and 35 Squadrons had moved to RAF Akrotiri in Cyprus. There they replaced four E.E. Canberra squadrons in the role of the Near East Air Force Bomber Wing to help maintain peace and stability in the area in support of the Central Treaty Organisation (CENTO). No.35 Squadron arrived first in January, followed by No.9 Squadron the following month.

The performance of the much newer Avro Vulcan B.2 meant that the two squadrons of the large delta could easily meet the task with which they had been charged. The Vulcan was better suited to night-time operations; its all-weather capability was another important attribute while the fact that it was equipped with WE177 provided CENTO with a nuclear capability in the area.

Two further Vulcan squadrons were declared to CENTO but remained based in the UK for reasons of cost. In addition to the Vulcans at Akrotiri, the island's air defence was provided by supersonic E.E. Lightnings of No.56 (F) Squadron.

For the next six years the Vulcans of Nos 9 and 35 Squadrons formed the Akrotiri Strike Wing until the British Government decided that, as of January 1975, forces would no longer be declared to CENTO, while the number of forces in Cyprus would be reduced with many being withdrawn to the UK.

The reasoning behind this move was that Akrotiri, as a British Sovereign base, would remain available to Britain, and UK-based aircraft would be deployed to reinforce Cyprus if necessary. This resulted in the Vulcans leaving Cyprus and returning to duties in the UK; No.9 Squadron took up residence at Waddington and No.35 Squadron moved to Scampton, where they became operational again on 1 March 1975.

In April 1976 NEAF disbanded and Air Headquarters Cyprus became part of Strike Command, the body that had been formed on 30 April 1968 when Fighter and Bomber Commands merged.

With the modification of nine Vulcan B.2 (XH534, XH537, XH558, XH560, XH563, XJ780, XJ782, XJ823 and XJ825) airframes to strategic reconnaissance standard, all of which it was intended would operate in the Maritime Reconnaissance Role (MRR), it had been hoped that the Vulcan would have a new lease of life as an effective long-range maritime strike aircraft throughout the 1980s. However, on the bomber front, it was found that the cost of extending the fatigue life of the aircraft during the proposed change-over period and the introduction of its replacement, the swing-wing Panavia Tornado multi-role aircraft, was too high, and so the decision was taken to phase-out all the Vulcans between June 1981 and June 1982.

No.230 OCU, which had been responsible for training all Vulcan crews since it had received its first aircraft in 1956, disbanded in August 1981 to be followed soon after by No.617 Squadron on 1 January 1982, No.35 Squadron at the end of February, and No.27 Squadron a month later. The intention was to phase out No.9 Squadron at the end of April and Nos 44, 50 and 101 Squadrons on 31 July 1982.

But then subsequent events in the South Atlantic in April 1982 put the remainder of the Vulcan disbandment on 'ice'.

7

Black Buck
(Operation Corporate)

The Vulcan's swansong came with the Falklands War in the South Atlantic in 1982, and the famous 'Black Buck' attacks using both conventional bombs and missiles. The H.P. Victor also saw service in the conflict in the maritime reconnaissance role, notably before the operation to retake South Georgia, but latterly, and more importantly, as an air-to-air tanker, a role crucial to the whole Black Buck operation.

In its twenty-five years of service the Vulcan had never been used in anger, so it was ironic that just as the final squadrons were being disbanded the Argentine forces invasion of the Falkland Islands occurred. It was 2 April 1982 and the Vulcan was called to war. Although ten Vulcans were earmarked for missions to the South Atlantic, only five (XL391, XM597, XM598, XM607 and XM612) were fitted with Skybolt strengthened hard-points which were essential to allow fitting of the latest ECM radar jammer. Pylons were hastily manufactured to permit the carriage of AN/ALQ-101 ECM pods under the starboard wing.

The Vulcan's conventional bomb-load was twenty-one 1,000lb HE (high-explosive) bombs, and it was not long before the aircraft were checked, readied to receive them and cobwebs removed from the airplane's in-flight refuelling systems, which had not been used for many years.

To prepare for the long flight, the aircraft received a number of modifications, including the installation of Carousel inertial navigation systems, removed from ex-British Airways VC 10s, and the addition of a Westinghouse AN/ALQ-101 ECM pod, normally carried on the low-level Blackburn Buccaneer strike bombers. All the modifications amounted to over 60,000 man hours of work at the normal 'peacetime' servicing rate but it is remarkable what can be achieved when the circumstances warrant urgency, as is demonstrated by routine engine changes which usually took two working days, and were now suddenly completed in nine hours.

Training of four crews drawn from Nos 44, 50 and 101 Squadrons (two crews) began in mid-April on air-to-air refuelling techniques and conventional bombing. None of the Vulcan pilots had experience in tanker formation techniques and it was decided to attach an air-to-air refuelling instructor (AARI) to each Vulcan as there was no time to train co-pilots. The instructor would sit in the co-pilot's seat on attack missions with planned in-flight refuelling replenishments and either fly the aircraft or supervise the refuelling. The co-pilot would take over for the bombing run.

From the very beginning the refuelling training was beset with difficulties. Leaks from the probe streamed onto the Vulcan pilot's windscreens so that they could not see forward, and there were major leaks which caused three double-engine flameouts. At first the problem was put down to the inexperience of the Vulcan crews in in-flight refuelling techniques, but after much investigation it was traced to bent spindles in the mushroom valves in the new Vulcan probes that had been fitted.

Preparations for the 1982 Black Buck missions necessitated intensive training in the taking on of fuel in-flight. Vulcan B.2 BB aircraft from Waddington practised for many hours over the English countryside with their Victor tanker colleagues from RAF Marham, Norfolk. (Mike Hooks)

'Wideawake' Airfield on RAF Ascension Island in the mid-Atlantic, looking decidedly sleepy in early 1982. The only visitor is an Air Luxor civil airliner. (RAF Special published 2002)

By May 1982 Wideawake had become one of the busiest airfields in the world, with the RAF's Victor tankers and Vulcan bombers taking part in Operation Corporate arrayed adjacent to the control tower. Many more military aircraft, including RAF BAC VC 10 transports, Lockheed Hercules, HS Nimrods and Harrier Jump Jets, used the facility en route to the South Atlantic. Vulcan B.2 BB, serial XM607, flown by Flt Lt Withers, is seen here arriving back at the airfield on completion of the Black Buck One mission on 1 May. (RAF Special published 2002)

Vulcan B.2 BB, serial XM612, completed in February 1964, served with Nos 9, 101 and 44 Squadrons until being modified for Black Buck and is seen here arriving at Ascension with Harrier sidewinder-equipped fighter jets already in residence at the isolated base. In all, five Vulcan B.2 aircraft were fitted with Carousel INS and prepared for use on the Black Buck raids. Four reached Ascension, and three were used on the six missions flown to the South Atlantic. (RAF Special published 2002)

Vulcan bomber and Victor tanker crew members gathered in the 'briefing' tent on Ascension Island, prior to flying Black Buck One. (*Take Off*, Part Works)

Handley Page Victor K.2 ground crew, in the early evening heat on Wideawake, prepare the in-flight refuelling tankers for their gruelling mission to get the Vulcan bomber to the South Atlantic. (RAF Special published 2002)

As the crews continued intensive air-to-air refuelling training, visual and radar bombing, low-level flying and astro navigation, the mission planners were narrowing down their options. At first seven 1,000lb bombs plus bomb-bay tanks were favoured, but finally it was decided that a full bomb-load of twenty-one 1,000lb bombs should be carried with in-flight refuelling en route. After a high-level approach, planes would descend to 300ft under the Stanley Airfield radar, and then 'pop-up' to 10,000ft for the bomb run.

The Vulcan training for Black Buck attracted a great deal of unwelcome attention from the British press, particularly after the Royal Society for the Protection of Birds voiced concern about the RAF's use of Garvie Island near Cape Wrath for low-level bombing at bird mating time. *The Times* carried a cartoon showing two birds cowering under the shadow of a Vulcan, with the caption, 'It's not the noise I mind so much as the droppings'.

Squadron Leader 'Monty' Montgomery and his crew were the first to depart for Ascension Island, a tiny (just 35 square miles) sub-tropical rock situated almost in the exact centre of the South Atlantic, where they arrived on 27 April 1982 by BAC VC 10 from RAF Brize Norton. On arrival 'Monty' was appointed Vulcan Detachment commander and his crew became the specialist mission planners. Wideawake Airfield on the island was soon to become the busiest airport in the world as the RAF flew in supplies to aid the task force already travelling south, along with equipment to support the planned Black Buck missions and based a squadron of Harrier GR.3 Jump Jets there to repel any possible Argentine attack.

Two Vulcans, XM598 and XM607, captained by Squadron Leader John Reeve and Flt Lt Martin Withers respectively, left RAF Waddington, Lincolnshire, during the evening of 29 April. Each carried twenty-one 1,000lb bombs, and each was refuelled en route to Ascension Island by Marham's H.P. Victors of Nos 55 and 57 Squadrons.

The following morning Squadron Leader Reeve's crew was selected as 'primary' aircraft, principally on the reputation of his navigator/radar crewman, Flt Lt M.A. Cooper. Later in the day, with no time to dwell on things, the twelve Victor in-flight refuelling crews and two Vulcan bomber crews crowded into the small tent that served as a briefing room on the island.

The local weather man began the briefing by talking about the upper winds en route: these were westerly or south-westerly at around 65 knots. Near 20 degrees south and 40 degrees south there were two cold fronts where thunderstorm activity was likely, with the prospect of turbulence at the heights at which the air-to-air refuelling was planned to take place. He was followed by the intelligence officer who told the crews that fighter interceptions at night by the Argentine Air Force were thought to be unlikely but to expect anti-aircraft fire from the 35mm Oerlikon batteries arrayed at the airfield.

The flight time from Ascension to Port Stanley by Avro Vulcan was estimated at over eight hours, so any attack planned for early on the morning of 1 May had to be launched the previous evening. By the shortest route the distance each way was 3,886 miles; it was at the time the longest bombing mission ever mounted in the history of air warfare (subsequently superseded by the USAF B.2 Spirit bomber missions launched from Whiteman AFB in America to bomb the Balkans in the 1999 Kosovo War).

Roughly an hour before take-off, the twelve H.P. Victor K.2 and two Avro Vulcan B.2 BB crews walked to their aircraft and in a temperature of 24 degrees centigrade donned their immersion suits and began to sweat. Apart from the co-pilots, few of the crews were in the first flush of youth; indeed, it was air-to-air refuelling instructor Flt Lt Withers' fiftieth birthday.

At 10.50 p.m. Ascension time (7.50 p.m. Port Stanley), at one minute intervals the eleven Victor tankers and one reserve started to roll down the runway at Wideawake Airfield followed by the two Vulcan bombers (one reserve). Operation Black Buck was on its way. It was soon

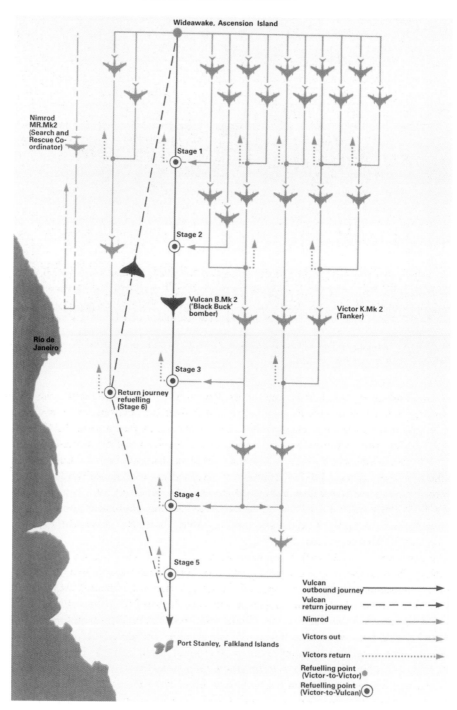

Wideawake, Ascension Island

Nimrod
MR.Mk2
(Search and
Rescue Co-
ordinator)

Stage 1

Stage 2

Vulcan B.Mk 2
('Black Buck'
bomber)

Victor K.Mk 2
(Tanker)

Rio de
Janeiro

Stage 3

Return journey
refuelling
(Stage 6)

Stage 4

Stage 5

Port Stanley, Falkland Islands

Vulcan
outbound journey

Vulcan
return journey

Nimrod

Victors out

Victors return

Refuelling point
(Victor-to-Victor)

Refuelling point
(Victor-to-Vulcan)

The complex route and refuelling plan flown by Flt Lt Withers' Vulcan XM607 for the Black
Buck One attack on Port Stanley. The bold line shows the track of the whole formation
over the Earth's surface, while the light tracks represent how the Victor tankers refuelled one
another on the journey south. (*Take Off*, Part Works)

H.P. Victor K.2 landing back at a wintery Marham Airfield following practice in-flight refuelling with Waddington Vulcan B.2 BB aircraft.

clear that both reserves would be needed. As they climbed away to the south one Victor crew discovered they could not wind out their hose to transfer fuel; the reserve aircraft replaced the Victor which then turned back. Squadron Leader Reeve, in Vulcan serial XM598, found he could not close the port direct vision window properly and so could not pressurise the aircraft. As they accelerated away, it became clear the rubber seal had broken loose from the frame and by the time they reached 4,877m (16,000ft) it was clear the only conceivable course of action was to declare themselves unserviceable and return to Ascension Island.

Flt Lt Withers was informed of the situation as he was climbing to altitude, and, after a moment's silence, he relayed the news to his crew. Avro Vulcan B.2, serial XM607, was now on its way to the Falkland Islands.

The first transfer of fuel took place about an hour and forty-five minutes after take-off, some 1,368km (850 miles) south of Ascension. Four Victors topped up the tanks of four others, then turned back. The remaining Victor tanker topped off the Vulcan's tanks but continued with the formation.

Already a problem had become apparent which could have led to the whole mission being aborted, the aircraft were using fuel at a higher rate than had been forecast. One of the reasons for this was that both types of aircraft were flying at speeds and altitudes that were not optimum for either type or for fuel economy. They were cruising at 10,059m (33,000ft) and descending to 8,230m (27,000ft) for the fuel transfer where the heavier Victors were more responsive.

When the first four tankers turned back they found that they had had to transfer more fuel than planned in order to fill up the south-bound aircraft, so much so that by the time they reached Ascension Island they were desperately short on fuel. The only runway at Wideawake runs between a mountain of volcanic ash on one side and rocky outcrops on the other, and can only be entered or left at the western end. The wind was blowing from the east and so the landing was to the east, with no exit and not enough fuel for an overshoot.

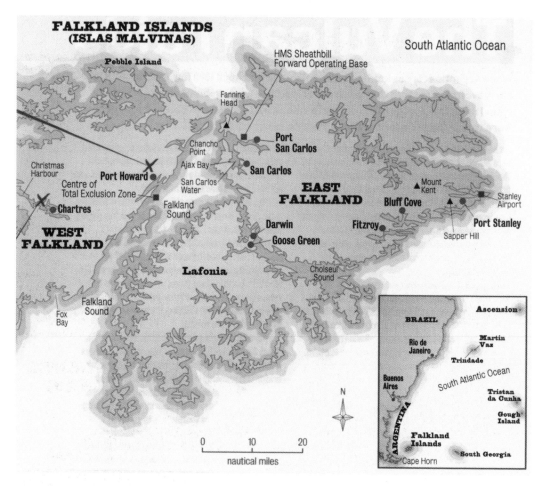

Falkland Islands (Isla Malvinas) and their relationship to the Argentine mainland. (*Jets*)

Argentine Air Force inventory and mainland deployments, April 1982. (*Jets*)

On arrival over Port Stanley, XM607 released its full load of twenty-one Second World War-type 1,000lb HE 'iron' bombs on the airfield. Unfortunately, only one scored a direct hit leaving the facility available for use by Argentine Air Force C-130 Hercules transports for re-supply missions, and also by the Pucara ground-attack aircraft located at the airfield, even though a number of the aircraft parked nearby were severely damaged during the raid.

Vulcan B.2, serial XM599, completed in September 1963, was not deployed on the Black Buck raids but served with Nos 35, 101, 50 and 44 Squadrons during its operational career until it was sold as scrap in 1982. (Mike Hooks)

Forty-five minutes after its first top-up Vulcan XM607 hooked up with its tanker again. When it disengaged the plane was 1,850km (1,150 miles) south of Ascension Island with full tanks. Immediately the Victor turned away and headed back towards Ascension. Soon afterwards Withers watched another two Victors pass fuel to the last three tankers before they too turned and headed north-east. The third transfer of fuel to the Vulcan took place after four hours. They were now 3,058km (1,900 miles) south of Ascension and after five and a half hours' flying, 4,426km (2,750 miles) into the mission, the Vulcan's tanks were topped up once again. By now the remaining aircraft had run into the poor weather. The thunderstorms and turbulence predicted by the weatherman at the briefing had been much in evidence en route, and it was during one of these that one of the last two Victors, captained by Flt Lt Steve Biglands, had to break contact when the tip of the aircrafts refuelling probe broke. Unfortunately, Biglands' tanker was supposed to be the one to escort Vulcan XM607 to the last refuelling point before the target.

The situation meant that the other Victor, XL189, captained by Squadron Leader Bob Tuxford, had to take back some of the fuel from Biglands' aircraft and escort XM607 to the target. Flt Lt Biglands turned north for Ascension. Meanwhile, XM607 formatted on XL189 to ensure that Biglands' probe was not stuck in XL189's basket. Having nosed up to within six feet of the basket, the AEO Hugh Prior flashed his torch onto the floating hose and it appeared to be clear. To make sure, Withers prodded his probe into the basket to check that fuel flowed okay. It did!

However, the time spent solving this latest problem meant that the three aircraft had continued further south than planned, and, in making sure Steve Biglands' plane had sufficient fuel to return to Ascension, XL189 had lost the reserves necessary to give away to the Vulcan if the Victor itself was to have enough fuel in reserve to return safely to Ascension.

It did, however, come as a profound shock when, about thirty minutes later, as the Vulcan was in the middle of its final transfer of fuel before pressing on to the target, red lights on the Victor suddenly flashed on to indicate that refuelling was over. The Vulcan was still 6,000lb of fuel short of what it should have had at this point in the mission. Withers broke radio silence with a brief request for more fuel, but Tuxford told him that he himself was now perilously short of fuel and that unless he could take on more fuel on the way back, his current fuel state would leave him 400 miles short of Ascension and likely to crash into the sea if no assistance from Ascension was forthcoming.

Later on, after the Vulcan had been heard to transmit its codeword 'Superfuse' for the attack having been carried out, Bob Tuxford was able to break radio silence to contact Ascension and request a spare Victor to rendezvous with XL189, and following replenishment the aircraft returned safely to Ascension.

By now alone, with the Vulcan somewhat lower on fuel than planned, Martin Withers descended to low-level when about 483km (300 miles) north of the Falkland Islands in order to start his run-in to the target undetected by radar.

At a distance of just over 40 miles the Vulcan climbed to 10,000ft and headed directly for the target. Having identified the target on the NBS/H2S radar, the aircraft proceeded on its attack heading of 235 degrees, whilst Withers concentrated on his heading indicator fed from the radar. Having been alerted by the passive warning receiver (that gave off a high-pitched tone at 10sec intervals), that they had momentarily been 'scanned' by an American-built Argentine TPS-43 Skyguard early-warning radar at Stanley, the Vulcan's ALQ-101 jamming pod under the starboard wing was immediately activated, and almost at once the enemy radar signals ceased. XM607 made one diagonal pass across the runway, on its attack heading, to release a stick of bombs at 04.46 a.m. local time. It took about five seconds for all twenty-one bombs to go. At the time the first bombs exploded the big delta was fifteen seconds into its 45 degrees roll to

Victor K.2 tanker XL189 touches down safely back at RAF Marham, Norfolk, following its important Operation Corporate deployment to 'Wideawake' when it played a major part in the Black Buck One mission. Aircraft captain Squadron Leader Bob Tuxford was awarded the Air Force Cross, following his heroic action that left him perilously short of fuel, but with Vulcan XM607 able to continue its long flight south to bomb the airfield at Port Stanley. (*Take Off*, Part Works)

port to make its get-away. There were no signs of jubilation aboard the Vulcan at this time, as the exertions of the previous eight hours had drained the crew of emotion and there were still seven hours to go to get back to Ascension, which was reached in the mid-afternoon of 1 May, after fifteen hours, forty-five minutes in the air.

Dropping the bombs diagonally across the runway was intended to ensure that at least one bomb would hit the runway and put it out of action. This was, in fact, the standard tactic for bombing 'long thin' targets – runways, ships, submarines and so on – with conventional HE iron bombs. This proved, (partially) to be the case. Later, reconnaissance revealed that the first bomb had landed in the centre of the runway, a second had clipped the southern edge, and another exploded between the airfield's only hangar and Pucara ground-attack aircraft parked nearby, causing serious damage. Whilst the hole in the runway was never completely repaired by the Argentines during the conflict, and although Hercules transports were able to continue to bring in supplies at night and the Pucara aircraft were able to use the runway, the damage certainly excluded any of the Argentine Air Force fast-combat jets from using the facility. In addition the Argentine Air Force Commander was forced to divert a significant number of his fighter assets to defend his bases on the homeland, in case of a Vulcan bomber attack on Argentina itself, although this had never seriously been contemplated.

Recovery of XM607 required four Victor tankers to fly out from Ascension, only one of which was planned to continue south, rendezvous with the bomber and accompany it back. Nothing was heard for some considerable time, but eventually an H.S. Nimrod MR.2 maritime patrol aircraft managed to assist in the link-up of the Vulcan bomber and the Victor tanker serial XL192.

The refuelling itself was not without difficulty as a leak from the Vulcan's probe caused fuel to spill over most of the bombers windscreen. But the aircraft did take on sufficient fuel to enable it to return safely to Ascension.

For carrying out the successful attack Flt Lt Martin Withers was awarded the DFC, and the rest of the crew (comprising Flying Officer P.L. Taylor, co-pilot Flt Lt G.C. Graham, Navigator Flt Lt R.D. Wright, Navigator/Radar Operator Flt Lt H. Prior, Air Electronics Officer and AAR Officer Flt Lt R.J. Russell), were mentioned in despatches.

For transferring as much fuel as possible from Victor XL189 to Vulcan XM607 during the final top-up on the south-bound flight, thus allowing the mission to continue safely, while possibly jeopardising his own aircraft and crew, Squadron Leader Bob Tuxford was awarded the Air Force Cross.

On the night of 3/4 May, XM607, deemed the most reliable Vulcan, again made the long flight south. The aircraft's bomb-load and target were the same as before but this time it was captained by Squadron Leader John Reeve who was forced to abort the original mission in XM598. However, this time the complex Black Buck One refuelling plan was revised. Instead of flying in one big formation, one wave of Victor tankers escorted the bomber while a second wave flew higher, therefore burning less fuel, with the idea that one tanker would have enough to refuel the Vulcan prior to its descent to attack the target and both would still have enough fuel to return safely to Ascension Island.

The same attack plan as for Black Buck One was carried out but this time the bombs were dropped from 4,900m (16,000ft). Despite extensive damage to the airfield, no bombs hit the runway. Vulcan XM607 and all the Victors returned safely.

This second raid, although of only limited success militarily, did serve to emphasise to the Argentines that the RAF was capable of continuing its attacks in the Falkland Islands and, if necessary, on the Argentine mainland. To this end the Argentine Air Force moved many of its Mirage fighters which had been deployed south, back to the north of the country to cover possible attacks from RAF Harrier jets forward-based on Ascension Island.

Black Buck Three was planned for 16 May, but was cancelled because of strong headwinds; this probably proved fortunate because by now the element of surprise had gone, and the Argentines were readying themselves for further attacks.

Having attacked the airfield at Port Stanley twice, the focus of attack now turned to destroying Argentinean radars operating in the Falklands.

Back in the UK at RAF Waddington, engineers worked to modify Vulcans to carry Martel anti-radar air-to-surface missiles. Although the trials proved satisfactory, there was concern with regard to the long transit to the target at high altitude and the reliability of the missile. The idea was cancelled when the Unted States government offered a supply of AGM-45A Shrike missiles to carry out the task and so modifications were made to the pylons to carry up to two Shrikes on each pylon. Suitably modified, on 26 May XM597 flew to Ascension followed the next day by XM598 in preparation for further Black Buck missions.

Black Buck Four, Vulcan XM597, captained by Squadron Leader Neil McDougall, took off on 28 May and was aborted five hours into the mission due to problems with one of the Victor tankers Hose Deployment Units (HDUs). Subsequently Vulcan XM597, again captained by Squadron Leader McDougall, took off at midnight on 30/31 May to fly Black Buck Five. The target was the Westinghouse AN/TPS-43F early-warning surveillance radar at Port Stanley. All went well throughout the transit south. Having approached the target at low level as planned, the Vulcan pulled up and, receiving signals from the radar, proceeded towards the target. Almost immediately the radar operators reduced the strength of the transmitted signal and the first run was aborted; it was forty minutes before the signal was acquired again by the Vulcan's radar, and approaching the target from the north-west, two Shrikes were fired.

The TPS-43F escaped serious damage, as the Argentine radar operators had shut off the transmitter in time to save the equipment from being completely wiped out, although one of the Shrikes caused temporary damage to the system. All the aircraft returned safely to Ascension.

Flt Lt Withers (facing) chatting with Squadron Leader Reeve after his safe return to Ascension Island following his successful, but not uneventful, Black Buck One mission.

Opposite above and below: Argentine Pucara ground-attack aircraft operated from Port Stanley Airfield during the occupation of the islands. A number were destroyed or badly damaged during the raids on the airfield in early May 1982, but, needing only a short take-off run, those that remained continued to operate unrestricted from the only partially damaged runway. The Argentines didn't even bother to repair the damage to the runway.

Following the first two raids on Port Stanley Airfield with 'iron' bombs, it was decided that an attack should be made on the Argentine air defence radars. Back in the UK at RAF Waddington, modification work began to equip the remaining four Vulcan B.2 BB aircraft to carry Martel, or Shrike anti-radar missiles, on the under-wing pylons. Westinghouse Dash 10ESM pods fitted to all six B.2 BB aircraft can be seen under the starboard wing.

Black Buck Six set out three days later with the same aircraft and crew; the mission carried four Shrikes – two pre-tuned for the TPS-43F and the other two for Skyguard gun-laying radars. The raid followed the same profile as before. When Black Buck Six was within about 9 miles of Port Stanley, the Argentine radar operators, by now aware of the Vulcan's tactics, managed to switch off the transmitter in time to negate the release of the Shrikes. A 'cat-and-mouse' game ensued for almost half an hour, until Squadron Leader McDougall dived towards the airfield to try and get the radars to 'illuminate' the bomber. The ploy worked and two Shrikes were locked-on and launched, one detonating close to the Skyguard fire control radar, killing three of the operating crew.

On the return flight home, however, after four hours' flying to make the final rendezvous with a Victor tanker, during the air-to-air refuelling the bomber's probe broke-off, leaving the Vulcan without sufficient fuel to return to Ascension. McDougall was faced with no option but to divert to the nearest suitable airfield – Rio de Janeiro in Brazil.

However, even to make Rio meant a climb to a higher level and, in a further attempt to reduce weight and drag, thereby conserving fuel, the remaining pair of Shrikes were fired, although one 'hung-up' and remained on its pylon.

As the bomber approached Rio de Janeiro several sensitive documents were 'ditched', while, in the meantime, much 'negotiating' had taken place between British Embassy representatives and Brazilian officials to obtain clearance for the Vulcan to land.

Clearance to descend was eventually received by the Vulcan's crew and, after some expert flying by Squadron Leader McDougall during a very difficult high and fast approach, the aircraft eventually touched down safely with barely five minutes' worth of fuel remaining.

Subsequently, the use of Martel was abandoned; instead the United States offered to supply a number of Shrike anti-radiation missiles, and two Vulcan B.2 BB, serials XM597 and XM598, were suitably modified to carry two Shrikes on each under-wing pylon.

The Shrike missile that had refused to leave the aircraft was removed and impounded by the Brazilians, but XM597 and the crew returned to Ascension on 10 June.

For his outstanding airmanship under extremely difficult circumstances, Squadron Leader Neil McDougall was awarded the Distinguished Flying Cross (DFC).

Returned to the UK at Waddington in 1983, Vulcan B.2 BB, serial XM597, of No.44 Squadron proudly displays its Shrike 'kill' markings and Brazilian flag on its nose. Vulcan B(K).2, serials XH561 and XH560, of No.50 Squadron can be seen in the background. Completed in August 1963, serial XM597 served with Nos 12, 101, 44, 50, 9 and 44 Squadrons until it was presented to the Museum of Flight, East Fortune Airfield, East Lothian, in 1984.

The last Black Buck mission was flown by Vulcan XM607 of No.44 Squadron on the night of 11/12 June with twenty-one 1,000lb 'iron' bombs fused to 'air burst' against airfield facilities at Port Stanley. Captained once again by Flt Lt Martin Withers, the mission was successful. Apart from an engine flame-out which took three attempts to relight, this final mission was uneventful and the aircraft returned safely.

Militarily, what the Vulcans achieved was strictly limited and they had little effect on the outcome of the war. But psychologically and logistically the raids were significant, both to the occupying forces, the British forces, and the Falkland islanders, as they underlined in the strongest terms Britain's determination to carry the fight to Argentina. It emphasised to the Argentineans the fact that the British forces could attack what it liked and when it liked. Subsequently, Argentina surrendered on 14 June 1982.

It is important to remember that over the Falklands throughout May 1982, during only two Black Buck missions (one partially successful), there took place some of the most ferocious aerial combat in the history of jet warfare. To take an example, in just one two-hour period in the late morning of 21 May, with both attacking and defending aircraft operating at extreme range from their bases, the Fuerza Aérea Argentina (FAA) lost no fewer than nine attack aircraft and three pilots in low-level operations against British warships. All of them were shot down by the AIM-9L Sidewinder missiles and 30mm Aden cannon of the Royal Navy's Fleet Air Arm (FAA)

Vulcan B.2 BB, serial XM607, again captained by Flt Lt Withers, lands back at Ascension Island after what proved to be, following the Argentine surrender, the final Black Buck mission on 11/12 June 1982. (RAF Special published 2002)

Sea Harriers. The FAA conducted their operations from the confines of the Royal Navy aircraft carrier's HMS *Invincible* and *Hermes*.

At this point we should refer to Commander N.D. 'Sharkey' Ward DFC, AFC (Rtd), who, in his book *Sea Harrier*, was highly critical of the RAF Vulcan bomber missions, first as to their military contribution to the conflict, and secondly with regard to the cost to the British taxpayer in terms of the massive amount of aviation fuel used in flying the missions for such small returns.

Commander Ward was also critical of the praise bestowed upon the RAF, and what he saw as their much exaggerated opinion of their own importance in the conflict; that role was, in his view, subordinate to the part played by the FAA Sea Harriers that flew the bulk of the combat missions, often in the most atrocious weather. As senior aerial warfare commander in the South Atlantic he was also highly critical of the reception he received from 'officialdom' and the RAF staff at their Brize Norton base in Oxfordshire following his repatriation by RAF Lockheed TriStar from the South Atlantic. It appeared to all present at a reception held at the base that the RAF had won the war, single-handedly! Or was it just a matter of old rivalry renewed, between the senior and junior service?

After the conflict, No.101 Squadron disbanded at RAF Waddington on 4 August, followed on 21 December by the disbanding of No.44 Squadron. By the end of 1982 this left No.50 Squadron at Waddington as the only remaining Vulcan unit.

Having retaken the Falklands there was a need to keep a military presence in the islands, with a continuous supply route to be maintained to the South Atlantic via Ascension Island which involved air transportation of both personnel and equipment. Now the RAF really was coming to the fore!

To make up for the loss to the RAF of a number of Handley Page Victor tanker aircraft, many of which had used up the bulk of their 'fatigue' life hours flying the Black Buck missions, and with a number of Victor tankers needed to maintain the 'air bridge' post-war, six Avro Vulcan B.2s (XH558, XH560, XH561, XJ825, XL445 and XM571) were converted to K.2 tanker configuration as a stop-gap, pending delivery of the BAC VC 10K airliner tanker conversions in progress at BAe Filton, Bristol. The six Vulcan B(K).2 aircraft were fitted with a single HDU in the rear fuselage and an extra fuel tank in the bomb-bay; No.50 Squadron flew with this equipment until March 1984. The first aircraft to be modified by British Aerospace at Woodford to single-point K.2 refuelling tanker was XH561, which was completed in June 1982 and delivered back to the RAF.

The conversion of the Vulcan to its new role was another 'twist' in the history of the big delta. For those who mourned the parting of the airplane from RAF front-line service – aircrew, ground-crew and aviation enthusiasts alike – it kept the Vulcan in the sky for nearly two more years.

Although the Vulcan K.2 proved a successful addition to the RAF's in-flight refuelling inventory, its days were numbered as, one by one, the Hose Drum Units were removed for fitment to the newly commissioned BAC VC 10K tanker aircraft.

Finally, the end of era came when, on 31 March 1984, the last remaining Vulcan unit, No.50 Squadron at RAF Waddington, Lincolnshire, disbanded and brought to an end twenty-seven years of distinguished service of the big delta. Or did it…?

8

And finally – FAREWELL

Avro Vulcan B.2s, serials XH558, B.2 (MRR/K.2) and XL426 B.2 BS were completed in June 1960 and September 1962 respectively. Both aircraft went on to have distinguished operational careers with front-line squadrons. XH558 served with 230 OCU, No.27 Squadron in the maritime reconnaissance role (MRR), and latterly with No.50 Squadron as an air-to-air refuelling tanker B(K).2

XL426 entered service on 7 September 1962 with No.83 Squadron; this role was followed by service with Nos 27, 50 and 617 Squadrons plus 230 OCU. XL426 has the dubious honour of being the 298th and last Vulcan to undergo major servicing at Wales's RAF St Athans, maintenance unit in 1981. Many more Vulcans followed XL426 into the maintenance facility, but no more ever left, as by now the spares recovery (i.e. scrapping!) had begun. XL426 also proved to be the last to serve in bomber configuration and took part in the last Vulcan 'scramble' in March 1984 just prior to No.50 Squadron's disbandment. For the next two summers it was the display aircraft of the RAF's Vulcan Display Flight that was formed within No.55 Squadron (flying H.P. Victor K.2 tankers) on 1 April 1984 until it was superceded in 1986 by XH558. The Vulcan Display Flight disbanded on 21 September 1992 at RAF Waddington, XH558 having flown its last display accompanied by the Red Arrows at Cranfield Aerodrome, Bedfordshire, the previous day.

It was in 1986 that XL426 was sold into civil ownership with Roy Jacobsen, and on 19 December that year it was flown into Southend Airport in Essex. On 7 July 1987 XL426 was entered on the CAA civil register as G-VJET. At this stage it had completed 6,236.1 airframe hours in 1,891 cycles. Southend had been chosen as the point of delivery because of a tentative agreement with a maintenance company based at the airport to maintain the airplane in 'flyable' condition. Unfortunately this fell through and it was unable to meet CAA requirements that called for the aircraft to be 'on the charge' of a major contractor with type-experience; it could not be flown to another airfield/contractor and so became 'marooned' at Southend.

A similar fate befell XH558 following its delivery into civilian hands and re-registration as G-VLCN at Bruntingthorpe Aerodrome on 23 March 1993, while the decision to sell XH558 to C. Walton Limited (Aircraft Division) of Bruntingthorpe Aerodrome, Lutterworth, Leicestershire, was announced by the then Minister of State for Defence, Jonathan Aitken, on 18 March that same year.

This brought to an end months of speculation over the future of XH558 following its final retirement by the RAF. Earlier that same day, during a meeting with the press at RAF Waddington, home of the defunct bomber, Air Commodore David Hurrel, Senior Air Staff

Escorted by nine BAE Hawks of the RAF Red Arrows display team, Vulcan XH558 made its final spectacular public farewell at Cranfield Aerodrome, Bedfordshire, on 20 September 1992. (BAE Systems)

Opposite below: At each location the bomb-bay doors opened to reveal the poignant 'FAREWELL' message to those who had gathered to witness the end of an era. XH558 had been completed in June 1960 and saw more than thirty years of operational service.

Above: On Tuesday 23 March 1993 Vulcan XH558 taxied out at Waddington for the last time before saying goodbye to as many as possible of the locations that had some kind of historical association with the big delta bomber, including its birthplace at Avro's Woodford, Manchester.

The 'Follow Me' Standard Vanguard pick-up truck in common use at RAF bases at home and abroad when the Vulcan first entered service, and indeed for many years afterwards. The Vanguard was a common sight on RAF bases at the time and the estate car was usually the Station Commander's 'pennated' official transport.

Officer of 38 Group, RAF, announced the Vulcan had been sold to the highest bidder and introduced David Walton as the aircraft's new owner.

Faced with a barrage of questions from the press, of which probably the most important was, 'what is the likelihood of the aircraft ever flying again?', David Walton's non-commital reply that, 'in the short term the likelihood of the aircraft taking to the skies again is somewhat remote, but who knows what the long term future may hold ?' did not leave anyone much the wiser.

Walton confirmed that the aircraft would be housed in the large 'Butler' hangar at Bruntingthorpe, built when the USAF Strategic Air Command Boeing B-47 nuclear bombers used the base. The plane would be preserved in its current condition and run-up regularly with all flying systems operating. Although, when questioned as to XH558's remaining fatigue life, Air Commodore Hurrell added that even though there were around eighteen flying hours left on the airframe, once XH558 landed at Bruntingthorpe it would be subject to all the CAA rules on flying ex-military aircraft and all the ramifications that entailed. The fact is, in practical terms this meant the aircraft would not be able to take to the air again without undergoing a major overhaul costing many millions of pounds, and it is sad to report that almost thirteen years later in 2006, there seems very little prospect of this, or of XH558 ever taking to the air again. By now, it is not just a case of finding the money to service the airplane, but also getting qualified personnel to do the job.

Squadron Leader Dave Thomas, former Vulcan Display Flight Captain, leaves XH558 at Bruntingthrope on 23 March 1993, prior to the aircraft's hand-over to its new 'civil' owner.

The retirement and delivery of XH558 to Bruntingthorpe Aerodrome created a great deal more interest amongst the aviation fraternity and press than did the retirement of its stable-mate XL426 at Southend Airport seven years earlier.

On Tuesday 23 March 1993 a strong cold wind was blowing across the airfield at Waddington, but this had not deterred hundreds (and maybe thousands) of Vulcan enthusiasts from turning up to see their beloved delta bomber take off on its final RAF flight from the famous Lincolnshire base. Just after 10.10 that memorable morning, the Vulcan's engines could be heard starting and running up. It soon moved away from its hard-standing near the control tower and taxied sedately along the perimeter track towards the assembled throng and the end of runway 21. After the customary final engine run-ups, it rolled down the runway to majestically climb into the air before levelling out over the base to make a low-level fly by. As it flew over the airfield the bomb-bay opened to display the famous 'FAREWELL' still emblazoned on its bomb-bay doors. This was a distinct feature at the aircraft's public displays ever since its withdrawal from service with the RAF had been announced.

The aircraft then left Waddington to fly over as many Vulcan-associated venues as possible, including Avro Woodford, RAF Coningsby, RAF Cottesmore, RAF Marham and RAF Scampton. At approximately 12.30 p.m. it could be seen over the twin towers of Lincoln Cathedral, bidding a personal goodbye to that historic city, inextricably linked as they are, to

Finally into 'civil' hands. Air Marshal Sir John Willis C-in-C Support Command hands custody of the bomber and its Servicing Form 700 to David Walton.

nearby RAF Scampton, and the famous 'Dambusters' who also operated the big delta from May 1958 until December 1981. Minutes later it returned to fly across RAF Waddington, its home for many years, for the last time, before making a final steep climb into the skies to fly the short distance to Bruntingthorpe.

Jointly captained by former Vulcan Display Flight pilots, Squadron Leaders Dave Thomas and Paul Millikin, it was Squadron Leader Millikin who brought the aircraft around for a slow approach as the runway was given a thorough visual scan. Then, with bomb doors open, the big bomber powered into its characteristic climb and wing-tip turn for the last time. Turning off downwind, before the turn and land-on, the final touch-down was arrested by the streaming of the large braking parachute.

The aircraft navigated itself along Bruntingthorpe's copious taxiways to come to rest in front of the control tower – where a huge crowd had gathered to witness the shut-down of the four R-R Olympus engines and the hand-over ceremony by Air Marshall Sir John Willis C-in-C Support Command.

The *Royal Air Force Yearbook*, 2006, reported that the project to return Avro Vulcan XH558 to flight was well underway at Bruntingthorpe. The engineering work and initial testing had provided better than expected results and Marshall Aerospace and Vulcan Operating

Co. teams are working hard to bring it all together for a test flight in 2007. Those wishing to monitor the restoration can go online (www.vulcantothesky.com) and via 'Vulcams' can view the activity in the new hangar. Could it be that a new chapter in Avro Vulcan B.2 serial XH558 illustrious career is about to unfold?

'Vulcan to the Sky'. Will Bruntingthorpe's 'Lady at Rest' take to the skies again in 2007 on the twenty-fifth anniversary of the Falklands epic flights? (BAE Systems)

Sources and Bibliography

Books

Ashworth, C., *RAF Bomber Command* (Patrick Stephens Ltd, Yeovil, UK, 1995)
Brookes. A., *The History of Britain's Airborne Deterrent V Force* (Janes, London, 1982)
Mason, F.K., *The British Bomber since 1914* (Putnam, London, 1994)
Thetford O., *Aircraft of the RAF since 1918* (Putnam, London, 1988)

Magazines & Periodicals

Aerospace Publishing Ltd *Take-Off* (Issues 15, 16, 17 and 26, 1994)
Air Forces International, *Vulcan Data File* (Modelaid International Publications, 1988)
Aviation Magazines & Periodicals, Various
Dancey, P.G., Personal Archives

Special Publications

A *Lincolnshire Echo* Special Publication, *The Vulcan*, 12 March 1994
RAF Special Publication 2002, *Second to None*
Vulcan Memorial Flt Supporters' Club, *A History & Guide to Vulcan XL426 'G-VJET*

If you are interested in purchasing other books published by Tempus,
or in case you have difficulty finding any Tempus books in your local bookshop,
you can also place orders directly through our website

www.tempus-publishing.com